# HOCUS POCUS!

## Halloween Crafts for a Spooktacular Holiday

Martingale®
& COMPANY

## CREDITS

President • Nancy J. Martin
CEO • Daniel J. Martin
Publisher • Jane Hamada
Editorial Director • Mary V. Green
Managing Editor • Tina Cook
Technical Editor • Dawn Anderson
Copy Editor • Melissa Bryan
Design Director • Stan Green
Illustrator • Laurel Strand
Cover and Text Designer • Regina Girard
Photographer • Bill Lindner
Photo Stylist • Bridget Haugh

Hocus Pocus!:
Halloween Crafts for a Spooktacular Holiday
© 2003 by Martingale & Company

*All rubber stamps used in this book have trademark
registration with the U.S. Copyright Office.*

• Flying Witch rubber stamp © All Night Media
• Bats with moon, "Happy Halloween," and Scary
  cat rubber stamps © Hero Arts
• 1¼" solid square stamp © Impress

Martingale & Company
20205 144th Avenue NE
Woodinville, WA 98072-8478 USA
www.martingale-pub.com

Printed in China
08 07 06 05 04 03          8 7 6 5 4 3 2 1

*Mission Statement*
Dedicated to providing quality
products and service to inspire creativity.

**Library of Congress Cataloging-in-Publication Data**

Hocus pocus! : Halloween crafts for a spooktacular
holiday.
    p.  cm.
Includes bibliographical references.
    ISBN 1-56477-491-0
  1. Halloween decorations.  2. Handicraft.
    TT900 . H32H63 2003
    745.594'1646—dc21

                                    2002156268

# CONTENTS

# INTRODUCTION

Greet the neighborhood trick-or-treaters. Carve the perfect pumpkin. Get gussied up in a crazy costume. Invite friends over for a fright-filled film fest. Celebrate the spirit of Halloween! The holiday offers a host of fun activities for all. And in Hocus Pocus!, you'll find ways to enjoy Halloween with the best tricks and treats.

This collection of decorating and entertaining ideas is sure to inspire a big Halloween bash. Lend your own brand of "spooky" style to invitations, etched glasses, and party favors. Delight your young guests with festive party crackers that open with a loud "pop!" to reveal a gush of goodies. Whip up candy-coated pretzels in the microwave, sew a set of pumpkin place mats with built-in coasters and napkin holders, or create a festive banner for the front door. Step-by-step directions make each project a snap, so even if you're new to crafts you can easily transform your home into a haunted hangout.

The magic of Halloween awaits, so—Hocus Pocus!—get ready to conjure up some spirited creations!

happy halloween!

Boo! Boo! Boo!

BY DAWN ANDERSON

# HALLOWEEN INVITATIONS

*If you're planning to celebrate Halloween with a party, make a customized invitation for those on your guest list. Each of these cards features a different Halloween motif. You can add your message to each card using an invitation rubber stamp, hand lettering, or a computer. The lettering for the witch card shown here was created on a computer, but use another method if you prefer.*

## WITCH INVITATION

## MATERIALS

- 2" x 2" scrap of yellow paper
- 8½" x 11" sheet of orange vellum
- Flying Witch rubber stamp (All Night Media)
- Bats with moon stamp (Hero Arts)
- Black dye inkpad
- Black embossing powder
- Two 8½" x 11" sheets of ribbed black cardstock
- Two 8½" x 11" sheets of orange cardstock
- ⅜ yd. of orange cording
- Computer and printer
- X-Acto knife, ruler, and self-healing cutting mat
- Keep A Memory Mounting Adhesive (Therm O Web)
- Circle cutter
- 8½" x 11" sheet of scrap paper
- Embossing heat tool
- Masking tape
- Keep A Memory Mounting Tape (Therm O Web)
- ¼" hole punch
- Two ¼" eyelets and eyelet tool
- Hammer
- Scissors

## INSTRUCTIONS

1. Beginning with a blank 8½" x 11" page on your computer, type the greeting "Happy Halloween!" and center it about 2½" from the top of the page. I used the Lucida Blackletter font in all lowercase letters. The first letter of each word and the exclamation point are in 36-point font with the remaining letters in 28-point font. Add specific details about the party in the area 4" to 6" below the greeting so as not to show in the window opening. Print the greeting onto the orange vellum.

2. Following the manufacturer's directions, apply mounting adhesive to one side of the 2" yellow square. Use the circle cutter to cut a 1⅛" circle from the yellow paper. Set aside.

3. Place the orange vellum on scrap paper. Ink the witch stamp with black ink and stamp the design onto the orange vellum, about 1⅜" below the Halloween greeting on the left side. Sprinkle embossing powder over the wet ink. Shake excess powder off onto the scrap paper and then funnel the powder back into its container. Emboss the powder with the heat tool.

4. Remove the backing paper from the yellow circle and position it on the wrong side of the vellum, above and to the right of the witch, to create the moon. The bat stamp I used had 2 bats and a

moon. To use only 1 bat, cover all of the stamp except 1 of the bats with masking tape. Ink the stamp with black ink, and then remove the tape. Stamp the single bat over the moon at an angle. Sprinkle embossing powder over the wet ink, shaking excess powder onto scrap paper and then back into its container. Emboss the powder with the heat tool.

5. Cut two 6½" x 9¼" rectangles each from black and orange cardstock. Cut the black rectangles so the ribbed design runs parallel to the longer edges. From one black rectangle, cut a 4¼" x 5" window opening, leaving 1⅛" borders on the sides, a 2¾" border on the bottom and a 1½" border at the top.

6. Apply mounting tape to one side of the black paper around the window opening and around the outer edges. Press the black paper over 1 orange rectangle. Trim off any orange showing around the edges. Using your X-Acto knife, ruler, and cutting mat, cut a window opening in the orange paper, ⅛" inside the black window opening.

7. Position the black cover with the window opening over the stamped design on the vellum, centering the design. Fasten in place, using mounting tape at the upper edge. Trim the vellum even with the outer edges of the black cover.

8. Layer the 6½" x 9¼" rectangles in the following order from the bottom: black, orange, vellum, and cover. Punch two ¼" holes, ½" below the upper edge of the card and aligned with the side edges of the window opening. Install eyelets in the holes using the eyelet tool and hammer.

9. Thread cording from front to back through the eyelets and knot on the back side. Trim off excess as desired. My cording had knots spaced at random along the length. I positioned the cording so a knot rested next to each eyelet on the front of the card.

# CROOKED TREE INVITATION

## MATERIALS

- 8½" x 11" sheet of orange cardstock
- 8½" x 11" sheet of orange mulberry paper
- 8½" x 11" sheet of black ribbed cardstock
- 8½" x 11" sheet of light orange cardstock
- 28-gauge black spool wire
- ½" orange pumpkin button
- ⅔ yd. of twisted black and orange ribbon (Mokuba)
- 8½" x 11" piece of HeatnBond Lite
- Iron and ironing board
- X-Acto knife, ruler, and self-healing cutting mat
- Bone folder or table knife
- Keep A Memory Mounting Tape (Therm O Web)
- Wire cutters
- Needle-nose pliers
- E6000 glue
- Scissors
- Black marking pen

## INSTRUCTIONS

1. Fuse HeatnBond Lite to one side of the orange cardstock; peel off the protective paper. Place orange mulberry paper over the top and re-cover with protective paper. Fuse in place. Trim the paper to 7½" x 10". Mark the center of the 10" edges on the solid orange side. Align your ruler through these 2 center marks and score along the edge of the ruler with the bone folder or the dull edge of the knife. Fold paper on the scored line to make the card.

2. Cut a 3" x 3½" window from the front of the card using the X-Acto knife, ruler, and self-healing mat, leaving 1" borders on the sides, a 2½" border at the bottom, and a 1½" border at the top.

3. Cut one 4¾" x 7¼" rectangle each of black ribbed cardstock and light orange cardstock. Apply mounting tape around the window opening on the inside of the card and around the outer edges on one side of the black ribbed paper. Center and secure the black ribbed rectangle to the front inside of the card. Center and secure the light orange rectangle to the back inside of the card with mounting tape.

4. Using the X-Acto knife, ruler, and cutting mat, cut a window opening in the black ribbed paper, ⅛" inside the edges of the orange cover window.

5. To make the crooked tree, cut 44 lengths of wire, 7" each, and twist together for ¾" about 2" from 1 end to make a crooked tree trunk. Separate the wires at the 2" end into 3 bunches. Place about 4 wires in 1 bunch and about 20 wires in each of the remaining bunches. Twist each bunch together for ⅜" to ⅞", then trim the ends, clipping individual wires at different points for a tapered effect, to make the gnarled roots of the tree. Use needle-nose pliers to finish twisting bunches tightly together at the ends. Separate wires at the top of the tree trunk into 2 bunches of 4 wires, 1 bunch of 5 wires, 1 bunch of 6 wires, 2 bunches of 8 wires, and 1 bunch of 9 wires. Twist each bunch together for a short distance to make main tree limbs, then separate the wires of each main limb into 2 bunches and twist a short distance to make side limbs. Separate larger bunches of wire again and repeat. For a realistic look, twist and trim each bunch to different lengths. Arrange branches as desired and press the tree flat with your fingers.

6. Close the card. Glue the trunk of the tree to the card back within the window opening, slightly to the left of center. Trim the shank off the pumpkin button with the wire cutters (see tip on page 63), and glue the button to the right of the tree. Allow glue to dry. Tie ribbon around the spine of the card and knot to secure. Knot the ribbon again 3" from each end and trim off excess.

7. Add greeting and details of party above and below tree embellishment on inside of card, away from window opening, using black pen.

# GHOST INVITATION

## MATERIALS

- 8½" x 11" sheet of orange cardstock
- 8½" x 11" sheet of black ribbed cardstock
- 2" x 2" scrap of light orange cardstock
- 1¼" solid square stamp (Impress B4547)
- Orange dye inkpad
- Ghost charm
- ¼ yd. of Boo! ribbon (Midori)
- X-Acto knife, ruler, and self-healing cutting mat
- Keep a Memory Mounting Adhesive (Therm O Web)
- Wire cutters and jewelry file
- The Ultimate tacky glue (api's Crafter's Pick)
- ⅛" hole punch
- Scissors
- Black marking pen

## INSTRUCTIONS

1. Cut a 5½" x 6" rectangle from the orange cardstock, using your X-Acto knife, ruler, and cutting mat. Write party details on the back, starting 1" from upper edge, using black pen. Cut a 5" x 5½" rectangle from the black ribbed cardstock so the ribbed design runs parallel to the shorter sides.

2. Ink the background stamp with orange ink and stamp the design onto the scrap of light orange cardstock. Trim the paper ⅛" from the edges of the stamped image. Apply mounting adhesive to the back of the stamped square, following the manufacturer's instructions. Center the stamped square horizontally on the black rectangle, 1¾" from the lower edge.

3. Trim the hanger from the ghost charm, using wire cutters. (See tip on page 63.) File rough edges with a jewelry file. Glue the ghost to the center of the stamped orange square.

4. Center the black rectangle on the blank side of the orange rectangle. Punch 2 holes at the top of the layered rectangles, ¾" apart and ⅝" below the upper edge of the black paper. Thread ribbon into holes from the front side. Twist the ends together on the back side and rethread each end through the same hole it was inserted into, pulling out on the front. Trim ends at an angle.

BY GENEVIEVE A. STERBENZ

# WITCH AND FULL MOON STENCILED DOORMAT

*The striking silhouette of a wicked witch flies past the ominous moon of an All Hallows' Eve. Simply made with spray paint, this rug is created using a stenciling-and-masking technique. The stencil is cut from cardboard that needs to be thick and durable enough to last through multiple coats of paint. It is important to apply light coats of paint from at least 12" above the stencil. This will preserve the stencil and give your painted images clean, distinct edges.*

## MATERIALS

- 2' x 3' brick-colored jute coir rug
- White spray primer
- Pale yellow spray paint
- Black spray paint
- Access to photocopier
- Pattern (page 13)
- Transparent tape
- Drop cloth
- X-Acto knife, ruler, and large self-healing cutting mat
- 18" x 30" piece of corrugated cardboard
- Newspaper
- Spray adhesive
- Mat knife
- Masking tape, 2" wide
- Kraft paper
- Clear acrylic aerosol sealer

## ◆ ◆ ◆ ◆ TIP ◆ ◆ ◆ ◆

When choosing a rug or doormat, look for one with a flat weave, which will allow you to obtain a clear stenciled image. Natural-fiber rugs such as the one I used tend to absorb some of the paint. That, in combination with the rich color of the rug I chose, can make it difficult to obtain a strong, vivid color from your paint. That's where the primer comes in: sealing the rug first with primer lightens the "canvas," so your paint colors will stay true.

## INSTRUCTIONS

Always use spray primer and paint in a properly ventilated area and follow the manufacturer's safety precautions.

1. Photocopy the pattern on page 13, enlarging by 250%. Tape photocopied sheets together as necessary. Cover a clean, flat work surface with the drop cloth. Lay the rug on the drop cloth, right side up. Place the self-healing cutting mat on a second clean, flat work surface, and position the

cardboard on the mat. Cover a third work surface with newspaper. Place the photocopied pattern, wrong side up, on the newspaper. Apply a light coat of spray adhesive. Turn the pattern over to the right side and position it in the center of the cardboard. Smooth flat with your hands.

2. Referring to the cutting diagram below, cut out the pattern around A lines only, using a mat knife for the less detailed areas and an X-Acto knife for the more intricate areas. Remove the 3 A pieces and set aside. Center the remaining piece of cardboard on top of the rug. Secure in place with masking tape on the underside. Apply a 2"-wide masking-tape border around the outside edges of the rug, leaving a 1" inner-border area of the rug exposed between the tape and outside edges of the cardboard. Cover the remaining exposed edges with kraft paper and tape in place.

3. Spray 2 light coats of primer from at least 12" directly above the rug. Allow paint to dry between coats.

4. To add the moon image, place the cardboard cutout of the witch and moon on the self-healing cutting mat. Referring to the cutting diagram, cut along the B line using a mat knife and/or X-Acto knife to separate the witch and moon images. Set the moon image aside. Position the witch piece on the rug, fitting it like a puzzle piece within the

larger rectangle of cardboard already secured to the rug. Place pieces of kraft paper over any small spaces between the witch image and the main piece of cardboard, and also over the 2 bat images and the inner border. Secure in place with masking tape. With only the moon area of the rug exposed, spray 2 to 3 light coats of pale yellow paint from at least 12" directly above the rug. Allow paint to dry between coats. Remove the witch piece of cardboard with surrounding kraft paper and remove the kraft paper covering the inner border.

5. To add the witch and bat images, place the moon image on the self-healing cutting mat and cut along the C line with an X-Acto knife. Set the C bat piece aside. Position the moon piece on the rug, fitting it like a puzzle piece within the larger rectangle of cardboard. Place pieces of kraft paper over any small spaces between the moon image and the main cardboard piece. Secure in place with masking tape. With only witch and bat areas and a 1" inner-border area of the rug exposed, spray 2 to 3 light coats of black paint from at least 12" directly above the rug. Allow paint to dry between coats. Remove all remaining kraft paper, masking tape, and cardboard from the rug.

6. Apply an even coat of clear acrylic sealer to the entire rug, following the manufacturer's instructions.

Cutting Diagram

—— Line A        —— Line B        —— Line C

BY GENEVIEVE A. STERBENZ

# HAUNTED HOUSE
# ICE BUCKET

*A galvanized bucket gets all dressed up for the Halloween festivities in orange-hued stripes and stenciled black accents, perfect for cooling down your holiday brew.*

*Galvanized buckets are inexpensive and commonly found, making them an ideal choice for an ice bucket. Their steely gray color might not evoke the same spooky feel as the rest of your Halloween decor, but with a few coats of paint and a stenciling-and-masking technique you can transform this practical item into a decorative piece you will use year after year.*

## MATERIALS

- 15" x 11" x 10" galvanized bucket with handles
- White spray primer
- Apricot spray paint
- Black spray paint
- Orange spray paint
- Drop cloth
- 220-grit sandpaper
- Tack cloth
- Low-tack masking tape, 1" wide
- Kraft paper
- Access to photocopier
- 2 copies of pattern (page 17)
- X-Acto knife, ruler, and self-healing cutting mat
- Low-tack frisket film
- Scissors
- Pencil
- Tweezers
- Double-stick tape
- Disposable aluminum pie tin
- ¼" flat paintbrush
- Clear aerosol acrylic sealer

## TIPS

- Be sure to press the masking tape down firmly and flush against the bucket, particularly at the edges to prevent the paint from bleeding.

- Use light coats of paint so as not to saturate the tape, which can cause paint to seep underneath and blur the pattern. Applying light coats of spray paint allows the paint to dry faster and helps to avoid drips. If the paint does drip, wipe with a foam brush, which won't leave brush marks.

- When using spray paint with a stencil, be sure to hold the paint can at least 12" directly above the stencil and apply lightly. Heavy coats can cause the paint to seep under the stencil and, when the stencil is frisket, can lead to bubbles. Exercise a little care and patience with this step and leave enough drying time between coats. A heavy hand with the paint will not provide good results.

- Always use spray primer, paint, and acrylic sealer in a well-ventilated area.

# INSTRUCTIONS

1. Cover one work surface with a drop cloth and place the galvanized bucket on the cloth. Lightly sand all outside surfaces of the bucket. Wipe away dust particles with a tack cloth. To mask off the interior of the bucket, position and press a strip of masking tape along the inner lip, flush with the top edge of the bucket. Line the inside of the bucket with kraft paper and tape in place. Line the outer base of the bucket with kraft paper, securing with tape. Trim tape flush with the edges of the bucket.

2. To prime the bucket, spray all outside surfaces with 2 light coats of primer. Let primer dry completely between coats.

3. Apply a light coat of apricot spray paint to the outside of the bucket. Let dry completely. Apply 2 to 3 more coats as necessary for complete coverage, allowing paint to dry completely between each coat.

4. Make 2 photocopies of the pattern on page 17, enlarging by 110%. Place your self-healing cutting mat on a second clean, flat work surface. Place 1 pattern on the mat and secure with tape. Using scissors, cut a 9½" x 12" piece of frisket. Center the piece, frisket side up, over the pattern and secure with tape. Trace the outline of the images onto frisket with a pencil, ignoring the outer borderline. Cut out the pattern with an X-Acto knife, cutting through both the frisket and the paper pattern beneath it. Lift off the frisket with pieces intact and set aside. Lift off the paper pattern. Remove all window pieces and pieces between the tree and the house on the paper pattern only. Center the paper pattern with missing pieces over the front of the bucket and secure in place with tape.

5. Using the paper pattern as a guide, remove one "windowpane" from the frisket, peeling it away from the backing with tweezers. Maintaining its orientation, position the frisket windowpane in the corresponding window of the paper pattern and press to the bucket to adhere. Continue positioning all frisket windowpane pieces and pieces between the tree and the house. Once all pieces are in place, remove the paper pattern.

6. Remove the center house and tree piece from the frisket pattern, leaving the border behind. Set the center piece aside. On the border piece only,

peel away the frisket from its backing and carefully position on the bucket, referring to the paper pattern for proper placement. Smooth the frisket flat against the bucket. Cover remaining areas of the bucket with kraft paper, using tape to secure in place.

7. Place the bucket on your drop cloth–covered work surface. Apply 3 to 4 very light coats of black spray paint from at least 12" directly above the stencil. Let paint dry between coats. Remove frisket and kraft paper to reveal the stenciled house, tree, and bats.

8. Place the second copy of the pattern on the cutting mat. Cut on the outer borderline with an X-Acto knife. Turn the paper pattern wrong side up and apply snippets of double-stick tape, particularly near the edges. Turn the pattern back to the right side and position it over the stenciled design on the bucket, checking that the pattern extends the same distance beyond the stenciled design all around. Press down to secure. Run vertical strips of masking tape around the bucket, about 1" apart, directly over the paper pattern. Because the bucket I used had built-in vertical "stripes" (actually molded ridges), it provided an excellent guide for creating the painted stripes. The 1" masking tape I used wasn't quite wide enough to cover the entire width of the ridges, so I overlapped two pieces of tape using the bucket's natural edges as my guide. Apply tape to the top and bottom lips of the bucket and to the bucket handles as well. Be sure all tape is flush against the sides of the bucket.

9. Apply a light coat of orange spray paint to the outside of the bucket. Allow to dry completely. Apply 2 to 3 more coats, letting paint dry completely between each coat. To reveal the pattern, remove all tape (using tweezers if necessary), the paper pattern, and the kraft paper from the bucket. Remove kraft paper from the inside and base of the bucket as well.

10. Apply masking tape below the top lip and above the bottom lip of the bucket. Spray black paint into the pie tin. Using the paintbrush, apply paint to the bucket rims and handles. Allow to dry, and remove tape.

11. Mask off the inside of the bucket and line with kraft paper as before. Apply a light coat of acrylic sealer to all outside surfaces of the bucket. Allow to dry completely. Remove tape and kraft paper.

Outer borderline

Enlarge pattern 110%.

BY LIVIA McREE

# ETCHED HALLOWEEN GLASSES

*Serve your guests their Halloween beverages in these spooky etched glasses. Choose a spider dangling from a web, a pair of pumpkins, or a skeleton hand. Translucent beverages show the designs off to best advantage. Make an entire set of one design or mix and match the designs as shown here.*

## MATERIALS

- Clear beverage glasses
- Clear adhesive vinyl (Con-Tact paper)
- Glass etching cream
- Newsprint
- Glass cleaner and paper towels
- Access to a photocopy machine
- Patterns (page 20–21)
- Masking tape
- Scissors
- X-Acto knife
- Rubber gloves
- Goggles
- 1" foam applicator
- Dish soap

## INSTRUCTIONS

Read etching cream manufacturer's instructions and follow safety precautions for working with etching cream. Work in a well-ventilated area near a sink.

1. Cover your work surface with newsprint. Clean the glasses using glass cleaner and paper towels.

2. Photocopy the patterns on pages 20–21, enlarging or reducing as necessary to fit on your glasses. Tape a pattern to the inside of a glass, cutting away excess paper as necessary.

3. Cut a piece of clear adhesive vinyl to cover the area to be etched. (Clear vinyl is used so that you can see the pattern you've taped to the inside of the glass.) Make sure there will be plenty of extra vinyl around the edges of the pattern to protect the glass from excess etching cream. Peel off the backing paper and apply the vinyl to the glass over the pattern.

4. Use an X-Acto knife to cut the pattern out of the adhesive vinyl while it is on the glass, making sure not to cut into the pattern. Remove the vinyl cut-outs; these will be the etched areas. (Shaded areas on the patterns should be left on the glass.)

5. Smooth the vinyl down to be sure air bubbles are flattened. Moisten a paper towel with glass cleaner and wipe the cut-out areas to remove any smudges.

6. Put on rubber gloves and goggles. Using the foam applicator, coat the cut-out areas with a thick layer of etching cream following the manufacturer's directions. On the spiderweb design, take care not to apply etching cream over the top edge of the glass.

7. After the manufacturer's specified time (5 to 15 minutes), remove the cream under warm running water. Peel off the remaining vinyl. Wash the glass with soap and water before using.

Top of glass

Bottom of glass

BY LIVIA McREE

# SPOOKY GLASS COASTERS

*Your guests will be delighted to place their beverages on these one-of-a-kind coasters. Stick with one motif for a matching set, or try all four designs as shown here. Each coaster is made by sandwiching a paper cutout between a piece of clear glass and a piece of orange stained glass. Before you begin this project, have your glass cut to size at a frame shop or hardware store.*

## MATERIALS *(for 4 coasters)*

- Black mulberry paper or other thin, black, decorative paper
- 12" x 12" piece of orange stained glass, cut into four 4¼" x 4¼" squares
- 12" x 12" piece of clear glass, cut into four 4¼" x 4¼" squares
- ¼"-wide silvered copper foil tape
- Access to a photocopier or tracing paper and pencil
- Coaster patterns (pages 24–25)
- X-Acto knife, ruler, and self-healing cutting mat
- Masking tape
- Glass cleaner and a lint-free cloth
- Double-stick tape
- Scissors
- Burnisher, such as a blunt wooden tool

## INSTRUCTIONS

1. Photocopy or trace the patterns on pages 24–25. Cut on the outer marked lines. Cut four 4½" squares from the black paper using an X-Acto knife, ruler, and cutting mat. Tape the outer edges of 1 black square to the cutting mat. Center one of the patterns over the black paper and tape it in place. First cut out all the white space in the design, starting in the interior and working outward—use the X-Acto knife and hold the paper taut as you cut. Next, trim the design along the outer pattern line. Cut the remaining 3 designs from black paper in the same manner.

2. Clean the glass pieces with glass cleaner; then position a black paper design on each piece of orange glass. Use a small piece of double-stick tape in the middle of the image to secure it in place. Place the clear glass squares over the images.

3. Use masking tape, temporarily, to secure the glass pieces firmly together. Start the roll of silver tape on the edge of one of the taped coaster units, but do not cut off any tape. Start in the middle of an edge rather than at a corner. Adhere the tape to the edges of the glass pieces. As you get to the masking tape, peel it off and continue with the silver tape. When you have completed all the edges, cut the tape with a little overlap, and burnish in place with a blunt wooden tool.

4. Cut 4 strips of silver tape, 4½" long. Starting with the edge of the glass at the top of the image, center the tape so that there is ⅛" of overhang on the top piece of glass and the side edge and ⅛" extending beyond the glass at each end. Fold the tape over to the top piece of glass and burnish. To finish the corners, use scissors to snip the tape where it creases, and then burnish the flaps down. Repeat to cover the remaining part of the edge, wrapping ⅛" over to the bottom piece of glass. Tape the edge at the bottom of the image in the same manner.

5. Cut 4 strips of tape, 4¼" long. Tape the side edges of the coaster, taping exactly from edge to edge with no overlap. Burnish all the taped areas well.

BY DAVE BRETHAUER

# HAUNTED HOUSE PARTY FAVORS

Create these whimsical haunted house favors to give to your party guests. Each paper house conceals a small papier-mâché box that can be filled with wrapped candies and other small treats. To accent the houses, ghosts were punched from white paper with a punch tool and attached at random to appear as though floating from the windows and doors.

## MATERIALS *(for 6 party favors)*

- Six 8½" x 11" sheets of brown cardstock for house
- Six black 1/8" brads
- 8½" x 11" sheet of chestnut cardstock for window backings
- Six 2⅜" x 2⅜" x 1⅝" papier-mâché boxes
- 8½" x 11" sheet of gold metallic cardstock for door backings
- Four 8½" x 11" sheets of black cardstock for roofs and window frames
- 8½" x 11" sheet of bronze metallic cardstock for shutters
- Wrapped candies or other treats
- Scrap of white paper for ghosts
- Access to a photocopier
- Pattern (page 29)
- Pencil
- X-Acto knife, ruler, and self-healing cutting mat
- Bone folder or table knife
- Incredibly Tacky glue (api's Crafter's Pick)
- ¾" x 1" ghost-shaped punch tool (McGill)

## INSTRUCTIONS *(for 1 party favor)*

1. Photocopy the pattern on page 29, enlarging it by 110%. Cut on the outer marked lines. Turn the pattern wrong side up and trace the pattern outline onto the wrong side of the brown cardstock. Cut on the marked line, using an X-Acto knife, ruler, and cutting mat. Mark all fold lines except for door on the wrong side of the cardstock. Position a ruler along each fold line and score with a bone folder or the dull side of a table knife. Crease on scored lines.

2. Cut along the door frame as indicated on the pattern, using an X-Acto knife, ruler, and cutting mat. Position a ruler along fold line for door on front side of paper. Score with bone folder or dull side of a table knife. Crease on scored line. Install a black brad for the doorknob to the front of the door, as indicated on the pattern. Cut a 1¾" square of gold metallic paper and glue to the wrong side of the brown cardstock paper behind the door.

3. Put the lid on the papier-mâché box and apply glue to the lid's outer rim. Wrap the brown cardstock around the box, starting with an end flap and keeping the lower edge of the paper and the box aligned. Apply glue to the flap and overlap the paper at the end. Press along flap to secure. Allow glue to dry.

4. Cut a scant 1" square from chestnut cardstock. Trace the windowpane pattern onto black cardstock and cut out using an X-Acto knife, ruler, and cutting mat. Glue the windowpane to the chestnut square. Glue the window to the front of the house above the door as indicated on the pattern.

5. Trace shutters onto bronze cardstock and cut out with an X-Acto knife, ruler, and cutting mat. Apply glue to only the inner edges of the shutters on the back and secure along the sides of the window, referring to the pattern and the project photo on page 26 for suggested placement. Allow glue to dry. Lift unglued edges up away from the house to create dimension.

6. Lift the house off the box. Fill the box with wrapped candies or other treats, and replace the house with lid over the box.

7. Cut a 3½" x 7" rectangle from black cardstock. With a pencil, mark the center of the long edges on the back of the cardstock. Align a ruler through these center marks and score along the edge with a bone folder or the dull edge of a knife. Crease the paper along the scored line to make the roof. Position the roof on the house.

8. Using the ghost-shaped punch tool, punch a ghost from white paper. Glue the tip of the ghost to the house as desired (refer to the photo on page 26 for placement ideas).

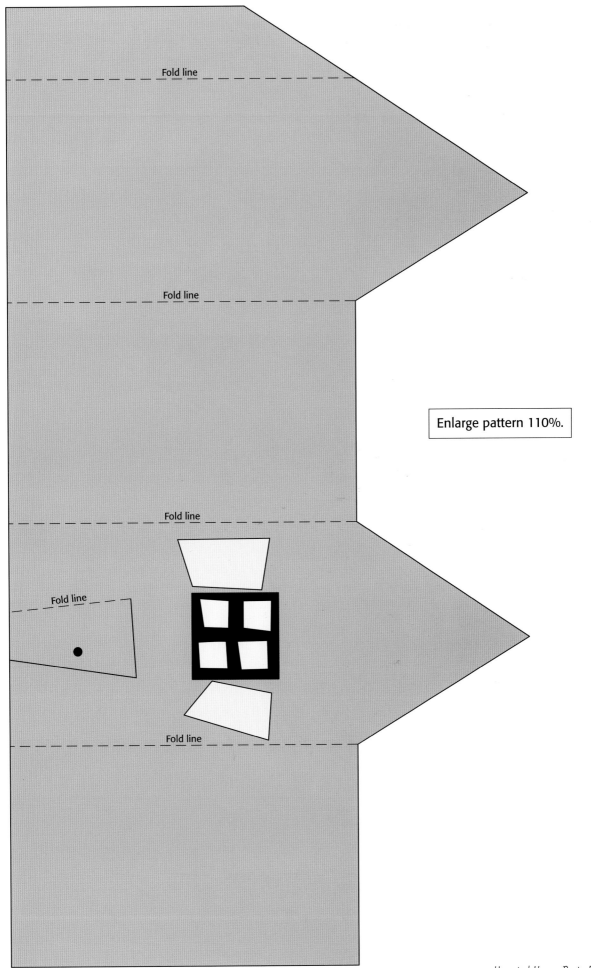

Fold line

Fold line

Enlarge pattern 110%.

Fold line

Fold line

Fold line

BY LIVIA McREE

# BAT FAVOR BAGS

*Treat partygoers to a bat bag full of goodies. These small gift bags decorated
with glittery hanging bats can be filled with candy, confetti, streamers,
and small noisemakers. Hang the bat favors from a fireplace mantel,
stairway railing, window frame, or potted tree branch.*

## MATERIALS *(for 6 favor bags)*

- Three 8½" x 11" sheets of black flocked paper
- Black ultra-fine glitter (Barbara Trombley's Original Art Glittering System)
- Twelve 4 mm ruby rhinestones
- Six 1¾" x 3" x 6¾" black gift bags
- 1½ yds. of ¼"-wide black organza ribbon
- Access to a photocopier, or tracing paper and pencil
- Pattern (page 32)
- White colored pencil
- Scissors
- Ruler
- Bone folder or table knife
- "Dries Clear" Adhesive with fine-tipped end (The Art Glittering System)
- 8½" x 11" sheet of scrap of paper
- Yes! glue (Gane Brothers and Lane, Inc.)
- Old ½" flat paintbrush
- ⅛" hole punch

## INSTRUCTIONS *(for 1 favor bag)*

1. Trace or photocopy the pattern on page 32 and cut out on the outer marked lines. Trace the pattern onto the black flocked paper using a white colored pencil. Cut out with scissors inside the marked lines.

2. Score the flocked paper on the wrong side along the wing fold lines, using a ruler and bone folder or the dull edge of a knife. Crease on the scored lines. Then, on each side of the crease lines and between the crease lines, roll the paper around a pencil to create dimensional curves in the wings.

3. Using the fine-tipped end of the glue applicator, apply glue around the outer edges of the bat. I applied a fine line on top and added more as needed for the glue to roll over the edge. Apply glitter over the glue, shaking excess onto scrap paper and then back into its jar.

4. Add glue lines along the wing creases and cover with glitter in the same manner. Allow to dry. Apply glue to the center body, outlining first and then filling in for even coverage. Cover with glitter and allow to dry.

5. Glue rhinestone eyes in place, using the pattern as a guide for placement.

6. Score the bag about 1½" from the top using a ruler and bone folder or the dull edge of a knife. Fold the top of the bag to the inside, creasing along the scored line.

7. Cut a scant 1¾" x 3" rectangle from black paper and secure to the bottom of the bag with Yes! glue, applying the glue with your old paintbrush. Apply glue to the back of the bat under the body area. With the bag folded and the flat side up (the bottom folded to the back), secure the body of the bat to the lower portion of the bag so that the bat conceals the bag's lower edge.

8. With the bag folded, punch a ⅛" hole through all layers, centered and about ¼" from the top. Insert ribbon through the holes and knot the ribbon ends. Fill the bag with desired goodies.

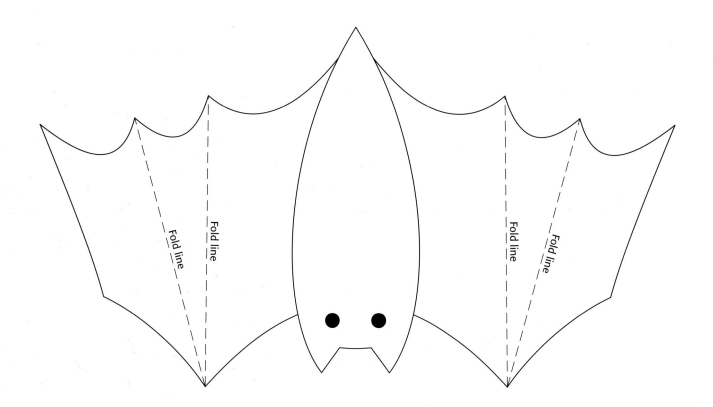

BY DAWN ANDERSON

# Halloween Party Crackers

*Bring a little excitement to your holiday party with these cat crackers. Each cracker consists of a length of mailing tube filled with assorted candies, confetti, or small gifts, all wrapped up with decorative paper and a snap. The snap is a narrow paper strip, about 11" long, that pops when it is pulled from both ends. The pop tears the paper wrapping and also elicits a delightfully surprised reaction from party guests. These crackers are decorated with a stamped Halloween greeting and a scary black cat with a dimensional button head.*

## MATERIALS *(for 6 party crackers)*

- Two 2" x 25" mailing tubes
- Confetti, wrapped candy, and small prizes to fill mailing tubes
- Decorative paper or gift wrap (This project uses black Thai Unryu.)
- 6 snaps for party crackers
- 5½ yds. of black-and-cream check ribbon, ⁹⁄₁₆" wide
- 8½" x 11" sheet of orange cardstock
- 8½" x 11" sheet of ivory cardstock
- Black dye ink pad
- "Happy Halloween" and scary cat rubber stamps (Hero Arts)
- Six ½" cat-face buttons (JHB International)
- Miter saw and miter box (or comparable cutting device)
- Rotary cutter, ruler, and self-healing cutting mat
- Pencil
- Double-stick tape
- Two 8½" x 11" sheets of Keep a Memory Mounting Adhesive (Therm O Web)
- Wire cutters
- Jewelry file
- Incredibly Tacky all-purpose glue (api's Crafter's Pick)

## INSTRUCTIONS

1. Cut mailing tubes into a total of 8 pieces, each 5" long, using a miter saw and miter box. Place confetti, candy, or other small prizes inside 6 of the mailing tubes.

2. Cut your decorative paper into 6 pieces, 7½" x 15". With a pencil, mark off 5" increments on the back of the paper along a 15" edge. Apply a 5" length of double-stick tape to the edge of the paper, centered between the marks. Apply a 15" length of double-stick tape along the remaining long edge of the paper. Place a snap on the paper next to the 15" length of tape. Press a mailing tube down over the 5" length of tape. Position the 5" lengths of mailing tube left over from step 1 at each end of the center mailing tube to shape the ends of the cracker. Roll mailing tubes from one side of the paper to the other, pressing on tape to secure.

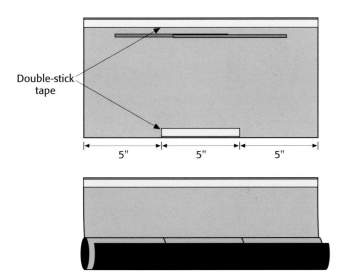

Double-stick tape

5"    5"    5"

3. Pull out the mailing tube at one end to create about 2" of space between the end tube and the center tube. Cut a 16" length of ribbon and tie it around the center of the space between the tubes. Tie bow in the ribbon on top of the cracker. Insert treats into open end of cracker tube. Tie end closed in the same manner as the other side.

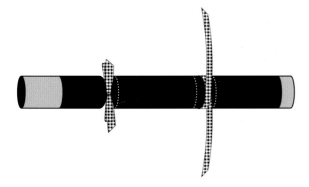

4. Cut 6 rectangles, 1¾" x 2⅞", from both orange cardstock and mounting adhesive. Apply the adhesive to the back of the orange rectangles, following the manufacturer's instructions. Set aside.

5. Stamp the black cat and "Happy Halloween" to the right of it on the ivory cardstock, using the black ink and rubber stamps. With the stamped designs centered, cut a 1⅜" x 2½" rectangle from the ivory cardstock. Repeat to make 5 more stamped ivory rectangles. Cut 6 rectangles, 1⅜" x 2½", from mounting adhesive and apply to the back side of the stamped ivory rectangles, following the manufacturer's instructions. Remove the paper backing from the ivory rectangles, center each one over an orange rectangle, and press in place.

6. Using wire cutters, clip the shank off the back of the cat-face buttons. Hold the cutters under the button so that the shank portion falls to the floor rather than flying up into the air. File rough edges on the back of the button with a jewelry file. Glue each button to the face of a stamped cat. Allow glue to dry.

7. Remove the paper backing from the wrong side of the orange rectangles and center a stamped greeting on each cracker between the ribbon bows; press into place. Remove the end mailing tubes.

BY DAWN ANDERSON

# CANDY-COATED PRETZELS

*These candy-coated pretzels are quick and easy to make. Simply melt white or dark cocoa candy wafers in your microwave, dip the pretzels into the melted coating, and then place them on wax paper. Once they've cooled you can drizzle them with a melted coating in a contrasting color for a fun Halloween treat.*

## MATERIALS

- Two 14-oz. bags of dark cocoa Candy Melts (Wilton)
- Two 14-oz. bags of white Candy Melts (Wilton)
- 14-oz. bag of orange Candy Melts (Wilton)
- 14-oz. bag of 3" pretzels
- 15-oz. bag of pretzel rods
- Microwave oven
- 9" x 13" microwave-safe dish
- Spoon
- Waxed paper
- 2–3 cookie sheets
- 2 forks
- 2 melting bottles (Wilton)
- 2 coffee mugs

## INSTRUCTIONS

You can melt your candy coating in a double boiler over the stove top instead of in the microwave. I chose the microwave method in order to use a long dish that was perfect for dipping the pretzel rods.

1. Empty 1 bag of dark cocoa candies into a microwave-safe dish. Melt in the microwave at 40% power for 1 minute. Stir with a spoon. Microwave for an additional 30 seconds, and then stir again. Continue melting and stirring every 30 seconds until candies are completely melted. Place a piece of waxed paper on a cookie sheet.

2. For 3" pretzels, place a pretzel into the melted coating and spoon coating over the pretzel until it's completely covered. Lift the pretzel from coating with a fork, letting excess drip off. With a second fork, scrape excess coating from the underside of the pretzel. Place pretzel on waxed paper to cool. Repeat the coating process for each pretzel.

3. For pretzel rods, hold a pretzel at each end with your index fingers and dip the pretzel horizontally into coating. Roll in coating until completely covered. Lift out and drag the underside along the edge of the dish to scrape off excess coating. Place pretzel on waxed paper to cool. Dip the back of your spoon into the melted coating and dab the ends of the pretzel rods to coat, if necessary. Repeat the coating process for each pretzel rod.

4. Follow steps 1–3 for each bag of white candies. Place half a bag of dark cocoa candies into a melting bottle. Melt in the microwave at 40% power for 1 minute. Squeeze the bottle to blend candy. Melt for an additional 15 seconds, and then squeeze the bottle again. Continue microwaving and then squeezing the bottle every 15 seconds until candies are completely melted. Turn the bottle upside down in a coffee mug so that candy coating fills the tip of the container.

5. Remove the cap from the melting bottle and drizzle coating over white-coated pretzels, moving the bottle back and forth while squeezing. Repeat the melting and drizzling process with half a bag of orange Candy Melts, drizzling orange over dark cocoa or white-coated pretzels. Lift pretzels carefully and move to another cookie sheet covered with waxed paper. Allow coating to cool and harden.

BY DAWN ANDERSON

# PUMPKIN PLACE MAT

Create this unique pumpkin place mat with a built-in leaf coaster and vine napkin holder. There's no need to save it just for Halloween—this elegant place mat can be used throughout the entire autumn season. The stem is set into the design, which can be tricky for a beginning sewer. The key is to mark, stitch, and trim precisely for perfect results.

To complement the placemat, try serving up a recipe of pumpkin bars, topped with molded marzipan pumpkins (page 42). And to finish off the place setting, make a Halloween wine glass charm (page 42). These simple decorations make it easy for each of your guests to locate their glass at a crowded table. Simply use a different charm for each glass.

## MATERIALS

- ⅝ yd. of green fabric for leaf, vine, and napkin
- ½ yd. of orange fabric for pumpkin
- ¼ yd. of brown fabric for stem of pumpkin
- ⅛ yd. of orange organza for facing
- 1 yd. of fusible knit interfacing
- Access to a photocopy machine
- Patterns (pages 43–45)
- Pencil
- Chopstick
- Thread to match fabrics: orange, green, and brown
- Sewing equipment and supplies: sewing machine, iron and ironing board, sewing shears, scissors, pins, hand-sewing needle, bodkin, point turner, dressmaker's marking pen, and dressmaker's tracing paper

## PLACE MAT INSTRUCTIONS

Seam allowances of ½" are included unless otherwise indicated. Change the thread color in your sewing machine as necessary to match the color of the fabric you are using.

1. Photocopy the patterns on pages 43–45, enlarging the pumpkin and long vine patterns by 200%.

Tape photocopied sheets together as necessary. For the place mat, cut 2 pumpkins each from orange fabric and interfacing, 2 stems each from brown fabric and interfacing, 2 leaves each from green fabric and interfacing, and 2 long vines and 2 short vines each from green fabric and interfacing. Cut 2 facing pieces from organza. For the napkin, cut a 19" square from green fabric. Transfer dots from the patterns to the fabric pieces with a dressmaker's marking pen.

2. Fuse the interfacing pieces to the wrong sides of corresponding fabric pieces, following the manufacturer's instructions.

3. Pin the long vine pieces right sides together and stitch along the long edges. Trim seam allowances close to the stitching. Turn right side out with a bodkin. Press. Starting at open dot, edgestitch toward the closest end, across end, and then along remaining long edge. Place the pumpkin pattern on your ironing board with the vine on top. Pin the vine to the vine placement line on the pattern at the open dot. Starting from this pin, steam and press the vine, stretching the lower edge and easing in the upper edge as necessary to match the curve in the pattern. When you reach the dot on the vine placement line, flip the top end of the vine over and continue pressing and stretching to match the vine outline on the pattern. If the vine stretches beyond the top edge of the pattern, trim the excess, allowing for a ½" seam allowance. Set aside.

4. Pin the short vine pieces right sides together. Stitch along both long edges and the angled end. Trim seam allowances close to the stitching and clip across the points. Turn right side out by inserting a chopstick into the end. Press. Edgestitch close to the seam lines.

5. Pin the leaf pieces right sides together and stitch around outer edges, leaving an opening at the end of the leaf stem and between dots. Trim seams and outer points, and clip inner points. Turn right side out through the opening and press. Press seam allowances to the inside along the opening. Slipstitch the opening closed and edgestitch around outer edges of the leaf.

6. Lightly transfer leaf veins to fabric, using dressmaker's tracing paper and a pencil. Set your sewing machine for a narrow, closely spaced zigzag stitch and stitch over the marked lines, tapering at the ends. Stitch side veins first and then the center vein. Repeat stitching over vein lines using a narrow satin stitch.

7. Transfer design lines onto the front brown stem piece using dressmaker's tracing paper and a pencil. Stitch over lines, using a narrow zigzag stitch, followed by a narrow satin stitch as before.

8. Stay stitch each pumpkin piece a scant ½" from the raw edges between the dots at the top. Position an organza facing piece over the top of 1 pumpkin, matching raw edges and dots, and pin in place. With the pumpkin side up, stitch between the 3 center dots, just beyond the previous stitching on the ½" seam line. Stitch just to the seam line at each end; do not overstitch. Clip the seam allowances to the stitching at the dots. Trim organza and pumpkin fabric close to the stitching. Turn organza to the wrong side and press. Repeat on the remaining pumpkin piece.

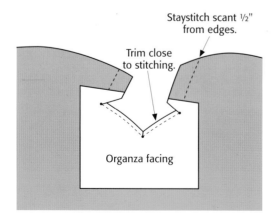

Staystitch scant ½" from edges.

Trim close to stitching.

Organza facing

9. Remove the long vine from the pumpkin pattern. Baste the vine and the leaf stem right sides together to the front brown stem piece at marked placement points, stitching a scant ½" from the edge of the stem.

10. Position pumpkin front over stem front, right sides up, aligning seam lines; pin. Edgestitch between the 3 center dots through all layers, moving vine out of the way, to secure in place; stop stitching exactly on the seam lines at the ends. Repeat with the back pumpkin and stem pieces.

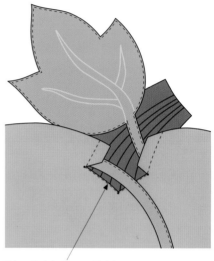

Edgestitch between 3 dots.

11. Fold the pumpkin piece over along one edge of the stem and align pumpkin and stem seam allowances, right sides together. Stitch between dots as shown. Stitch from dot to dot and do not overstitch; backstitch at ends. Repeat on the other side of the stem. Clip the seam allowance to dots at the top of the pumpkin. Trim seam allowances below dots and press toward the stem. Repeat on the back pumpkin and stem pieces.

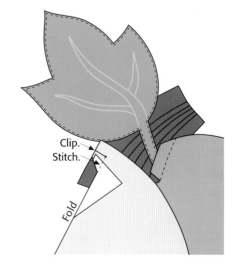

Clip.
Stitch.
Fold

12. Pin the pumpkin front to the pumpkin back, right sides together, keeping the vine and leaf away from outer seam lines. Stitch around the pumpkin from dot to dot, leaving an opening between dots as indicated on the pattern and keeping the stem out of the way. Backstitch at dots and break stitching.

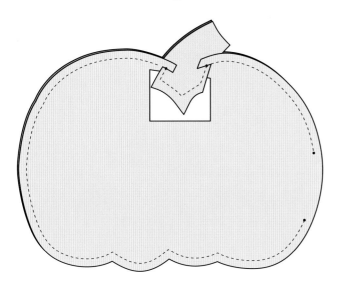

13. Move pumpkin seam allowances out of the way and stitch around the stem from dot to dot, between clip marks; backstitch at ends and do not overstich. Trim seams around pumpkin and stem close to stitching. Clip inner corners and trim across corners of the stem.

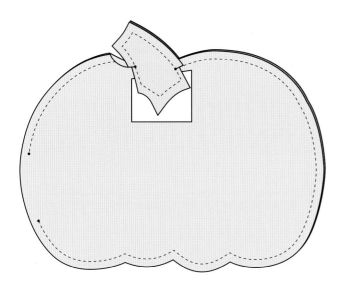

14. Turn the pumpkin right side out through the opening and press. Press seam allowances to the inside along the opening. Slipstitch the opening closed. Edgestitch around the outer edges of the pumpkin.

15. Lightly transfer interior pumpkin lines to the pumpkin front using dressmaker's tracing paper and pencil. Set your sewing machine for a narrow, closely spaced zigzag stitch and stitch over the marked lines, tapering at the ends. Stitch over lines again using a machine satin stitch.

16. Pin the vine to the pumpkin from stem to dot, using the pattern as a guide. Turn the vine over at the dot and continue pinning to the pumpkin until you reach the open dot, using the pattern as a guide. Edgestitch along the inner edge of the vine from stem to dot, tapering stitching off vine at the dot. Pull thread tails to the back side and knot. Thread them through your needle, and take a stitch into fabric between the layers, exiting about ¾" away. Trim off excess thread tails. Fold the vine to the right, out of the way, and continue edgestitching, this time along the top edge of the vine between dots. Stop stitching, pull threads to the back side, and finish off as before.

17. Loop the remainder of the vine around in a circle until the end meets the stitched vine at the open dot. Hand stitch in place.

18. Turn in ¼" on the raw edge of the short vine. Insert under the vine loop, butting the vine pieces together, and hand or machine stitch in place.

## NAPKIN INSTRUCTIONS

Press under ¼" on each side of the 19" square napkin fabric. Press under ¼" again. Unfold. Refold each side one at a time, and stitch along the inner fold from end to end, backstitching at each end.

# PUMPKIN BARS

## INGREDIENTS

- 1 c. oil
- 4 eggs
- 1 c. coconut
- 1 tsp. soda
- 2 c. flour
- 2 c. sugar
- 2 c. pumpkin
- 1½ tsp. cinnamon
- ½ tsp. baking powder

Preheat oven to 350°. Coat inside of two 9" x 13" baking pans with oil and flour. Blend all ingredients in a large mixing bowl. Pour into baking pans and bake for approximately 30 minutes. Remove from oven when toothpick inserted into middle comes out clean. Allow to cool. Top with cream cheese frosting (below).

## CREAM CHEESE FROSTING INGREDIENTS

- 6 oz. softened cream cheese
- 1½ sticks softened butter
- 2 tsp. milk
- 2 tsp. vanilla
- 4 c. powdered sugar

Beat cream cheese and butter together. Add the remaining ingredients and beat until smooth and creamy.

 ## DECORATING TIP

After frosting the bars, drag a cake-decorating comb across the top of the frosting to make decorative ridges. Top bars with mini half-pumpkins made with colored marzipan and a plastic candy mold. To make the half-pumpkin decorations, add a small amount of orange food coloring into marzipan with a toothpick and knead together until well blended. Repeat until desired color is achieved. Repeat with additional marzipan and green food coloring for stems and vines. Press orange marzipan into plastic pumpkin candy mold and press green marzipan into stem portion of mold. Place in freezer until set. Remove mold from freezer and remove half-pumpkin with toothpick. Place a pumpkin atop each bar. Roll a small amount of green marzipan between your thumb and forefinger to make a very tiny vine. Make a curl in vine, trim excess, and set vine next to stem of pumpkin.

# HALLOWEEN WINE GLASS CHARM

## MATERIALS

- 3½" of 28-gauge spool wire
- About 25 assorted small beads
- Halloween charm
- Jump ring
- Wire cutter
- Round-nose pliers
- Needle-nose pliers

## INSTRUCTIONS

1. Make a double loop at one end of wire with round-nose pliers. Thread beads onto wire for about 2¾". Make another double loop in wire at the remaining end, trimming off excess with wire cutters.

2. Open the jump ring with needle-nose pliers. Place the loop of the charm onto the jump ring. Attach the jump ring to the center of the beaded wire and close the ends to secure. Bend the beaded wire into a circle.

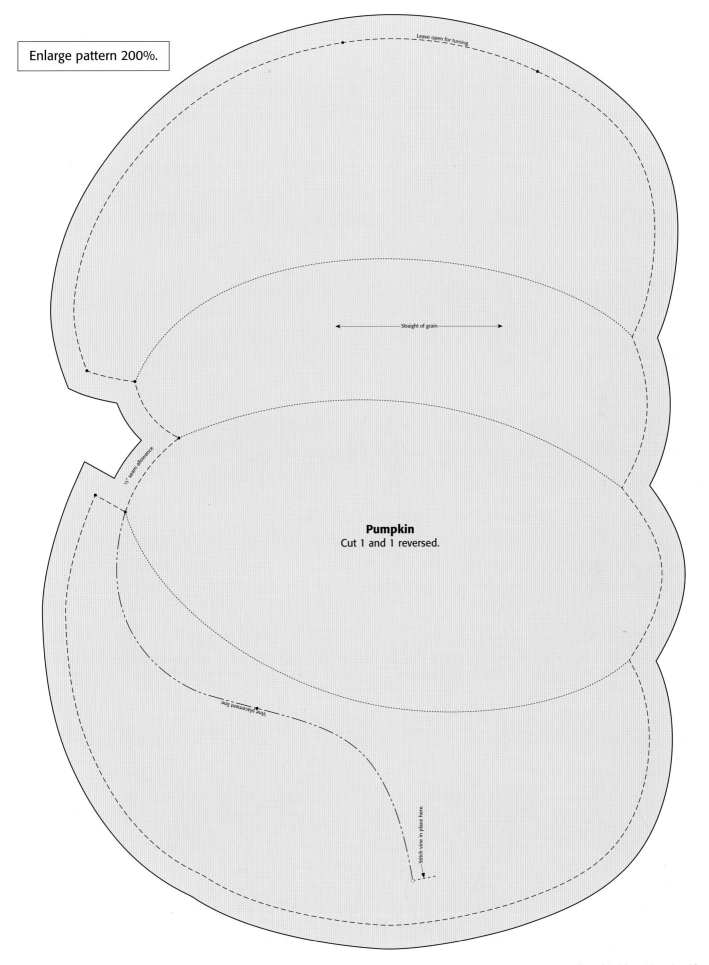

Enlarge pattern 200%.

Leave open for turning

Straight of grain

½" seam allowance

**Pumpkin**
Cut 1 and 1 reversed.

Vine placement line

Stitch vine in place here.

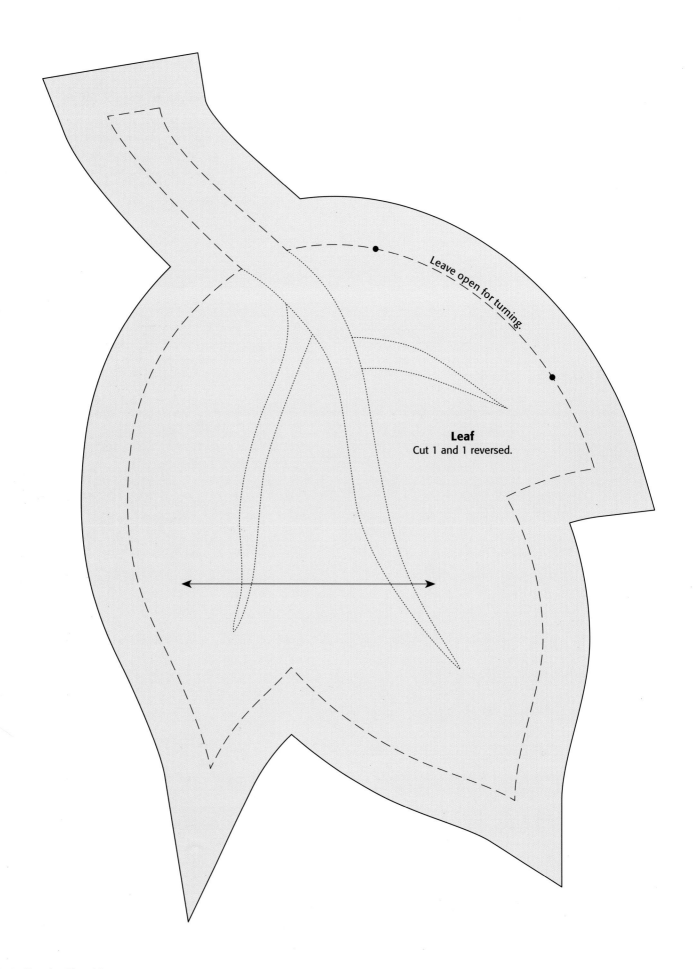

Leave open for turning.

**Leaf**
Cut 1 and 1 reversed.

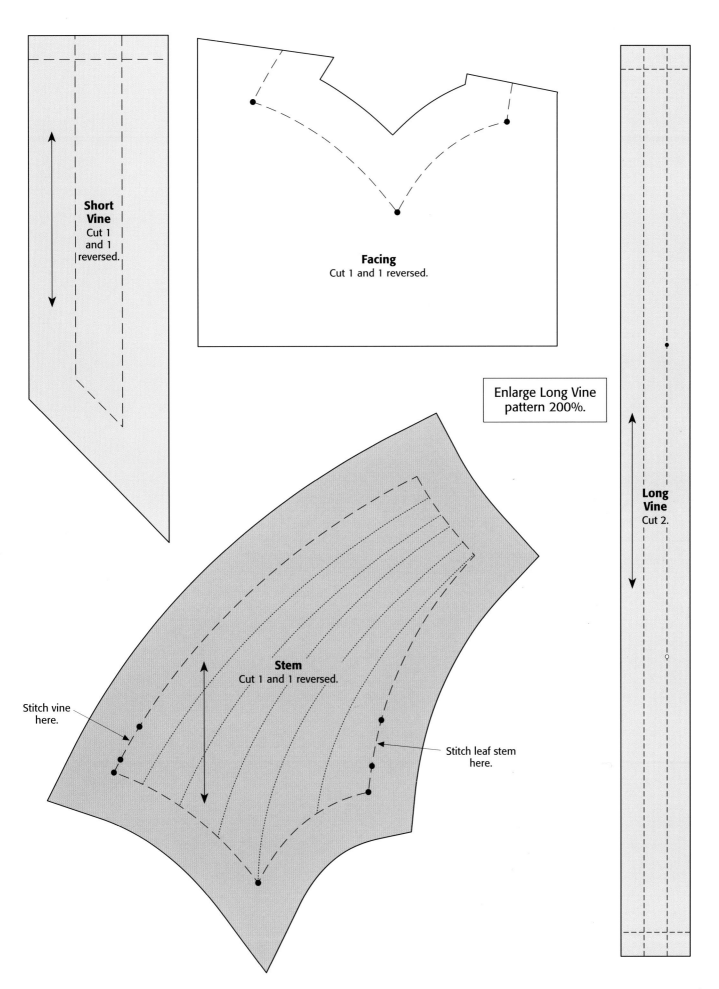

**Short Vine**
Cut 1 and 1 reversed.

**Facing**
Cut 1 and 1 reversed.

Enlarge Long Vine pattern 200%.

**Long Vine**
Cut 2.

**Stem**
Cut 1 and 1 reversed.

Stitch vine here.

Stitch leaf stem here.

BY SHEILA HAYNES RAUEN

# PAINTED CAT AND PUMPKIN TRAY

*Enjoy serving your Halloween party guests with this whimsical cat and pumpkin tray. Once the pattern is transferred to the wooden tray, you simply fill in each area with the appropriate color of paint. The background stars are easily added with a foam stamp, and then a few simple hand-painted details are added to finish off the design. Once the tray is sealed it can be wiped clean with water and a mild soap after each use.*

*For the perfect decoration to coordinate with the tray, try the Jack-O'-Lantern Ornaments (page 50). These little pumpkins are easily made with a few scraps of felt and a hand-worked buttonhole stitch.*

## MATERIALS

- Gesso (optional)
- 12½" x 20½" wooden tray (Oval Home Tray from Walnut Hollow)
- Delta Ceramcoat Acrylic Paint in the following colors: Purple, Yellow, White, Black, Tangerine, Seminole Green, Spice Brown, and Forest Green
- Jacquard's Lumiere Paint: Metallic Gold, Metallic Russet, and Metallic Silver
- 1⅛" star-shaped foam stamp
- Delta Ceramcoat Exterior/Interior Varnish in Matte and Gloss
- Newsprint or drop cloth
- 220-grit sandpaper
- Spray mister and paper towels
- Access to a photocopier
- Pattern (page 51)
- Paintbrushes (Loew-Cornell):
    - 2" gesso #1177 Nylon
    - American Painter Series 4550 1" wash
    - American Painter Series 4000 #0 and #4 round
    - La Corneille Golden Taklon Series 7300 #10 shader
    - Mixtique Series 8350 #00 liner
    - Series 797-F Flat stain #4
    - 1" foam brush
- Transparent tape
- Scissors
- Graphite paper
- #2 pencil
- Paint palette or disposable plate (for mixing paints)
- Disposable dish

# ◆ ◆ ◆ ◆ TIPS ◆ ◆ ◆ ◆

◆ Some paint colors may require two coats for total coverage. Allow the paint to dry between coats. The paint dries quickly, but be sure to let one color of paint dry completely before painting a detail over it with another color.

◆ Wash brushes thoroughly before using the same brush for a different color of paint.

◆ Whenever applying paint glazes (transparent washes), such as on the pumpkin, or when doing line work, such as the swirls in the background or the fur lines in the cat, dilute the paint with water so that it flows more easily.

## INSTRUCTIONS

The tray was prepared by applying a thin coat of gesso to seal the wood. Some artists do not seal the wood before painting. This is a matter of choice.

1. Cover your work surface with newsprint or a drop cloth. Using the gesso brush, apply a thin coat of gesso to the front of the tray. Allow to dry.

Repeat for the back and edges of the tray. Lightly sand the tray and remove sanding dust with a lightly misted paper towel.

2. Photocopy the pattern on page 51, enlarging by 150%. Tape photocopied sheets together as necessary. Trim the paper close to the outer edges of the design.

3. Place the graphite paper over the front of the tray and place the pattern on top, positioning the cat as shown on the color plan below. Trace the pattern lines with a pencil to transfer the design to the tray.

4. Using the 1" wash brush, paint the background on the front of the tray Purple, leaving the cat and pumpkin unpainted. Overlap the edges of the cat slightly. The fur detail will be added later. Allow the paint to dry. Paint the back and sides of the tray Purple and allow to dry.

5. Using the #4 round brush, paint the eyes of the cat and the facial features of the pumpkin Yellow. Paint the cat's teeth White.

6. Using the #10 shader brush, paint the cat Black. For this base coat, paint a smooth outline all around the cat. The fur detail will be added later.

Color Plan

Using the #4 round brush, paint the pumpkin and cat eyes Black. Using the #4 shader brush, paint the edge of the tray Black.

7. Using the #4 round brush, paint the cat's nose and the pumpkin Tangerine. Using the same brush, paint the pumpkin leaves Seminole Green.

8. Using the #0 round brush, paint the pumpkin and leaf stems Spice Brown. Using the liner brush, outline the pumpkin's eyes, nose, mouth, and teeth with Spice Brown.

9. Using the foam brush, apply a thin coat of Metallic Gold paint to the star stamp, and stamp stars in a random pattern onto the background. Reapply paint to the stamp for each star.

10. Using the liner brush and Metallic Russet paint, add dots at the tip of each star point. Using the #4 flat brush, paint vertical ¼" lines around the edge of the tray with Metallic Russet to create a checked look.

11. Mix a light orange glaze for the pumpkin by adding a small amount of Tangerine to White, and then mixing in a small amount of water. Referring to the project photo on page 46 and using the shader brush, paint the highlights onto the pumpkin.

12. Mix a dark orange glaze for the pumpkin by adding a small amount of Spice Brown to Tangerine, and then mixing in a small amount of water. Using the shader brush, paint shadows on the pumpkin around the outer edges and add two arcing lines vertically through the pumpkin (refer to the pattern on page 51).

13. Using the liner brush, add fur details to the outline of the cat with diluted Black paint.

14. Mix a small amount of Black paint to the White paint to get gray. Outline the cat's nose and mouth using the liner brush and the gray paint. Dilute the same gray and use the liner brush to paint the fur details in the interior of the cat's body. Also outline the cat's body and add the lines to the feet and the details on the ears.

15. Outline the cat's eyes with Metallic Silver, leaving an inner outline of black. Outline the top of the nose and paint on the whiskers with Metallic Silver.

16. Using the liner brush and diluted Black paint, paint the swirls in the background of the tray (see the color plan on page 48). Referring to the pattern, paint lines of Black between the cat's teeth.

17. Using the liner brush, paint veins on the leaves with Forest Green (refer to the pattern for placement).

18. Using the liner brush and Seminole Green paint, add the pumpkin vines (refer to the pattern for placement).

19. Mix a small amount of Black into Purple, and then mix with water to create a wash. Using the #4 round brush, paint this wash below the cat and the pumpkin to create a shadow, as shown in the project photo.

20. Using the liner brush, paint the highlights of the cat's eyes with White.

21. Mix equal amounts of gloss and matte varnish together in a disposable dish to make a satin varnish. Using the 2" nylon brush, apply 2 to 3 coats of satin varnish to the front and back of the tray, sanding lightly and allowing to dry between coats.

# JACK-O'-LANTERN ORNAMENTS

## MATERIALS *(for 5 ornaments)*

- ⅛ yd. or two 9" x 12" rectangles of orange felt
- Scrap of black for eyes
- Scrap of yellow for eyes, nose, and mouth
- Scrap of brown for stem
- Scrap of green for leaf
- Scrap of Steam A Seam 2
- Black embroidery floss
- 10 pearl-white size 10 seed beads for highlights in eyes
- Black beading thread
- Embroidery needle
- Beading needle
- Scraps of polyester fiberfill
- 28-gauge green spool wire for vine
- Wire cutter
- Pencil

## INSTRUCTIONS

1. Trace or photocopy the patterns for the pumpkin, leaf, and stem below. For each ornament, cut 2 pumpkins from the orange felt, 1 stem from the brown felt, and 1 leaf from the green felt.

2. Trace the pumpkin's eyes (both the outer and inner circles), nose, mouth, and one stem in reverse onto paper side of Steam A Seam 2, leaving ¼" to ½" around the drawn areas. Cut around the shapes, leaving the allowance.

3. Following the manufacturer's instructions, remove the protective backing paper. Referring to the project photo for color placement, press each shape by hand to the appropriate-color felt. Cut out the pieces on the drawn lines, and then remove the paper backing.

4. Place the facial features in position on one of the pumpkin pieces and fuse into place.

5. Using 2 strands of embroidery floss and an embroidery needle, outline the outer eyes, the nose, and the mouth using a buttonhole stitch (see page 54). Tack the inner eyes in place with running stitches. Sew pearl-white seed beads to the eyes to give them sparkle.

6. Place the stem pieces together, fusible side sandwiched between the layers, and fuse in place. Position the stem and leaf piece between dots at the top of the pumpkin and fuse in place on the back with small pieces of Steam A Seam 2.

7. Place pumpkin front and back wrong sides together and buttonhole stitch around the outer edges, stopping about 1½" from the starting point. Stuff with polyester fiberfill, and then continue buttonhole stitching around the remainder of the pumpkin. Insert 5" length of green wire at one dot and exit at remaining dot. Curl ends around pencil to make vine. Trim and shape as desired.

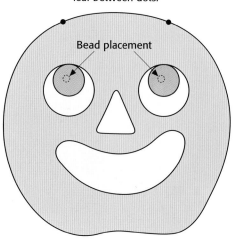

Insert pumpkin stem and leaf between dots.

Bead placement

**Pumpkin**
Cut 2 orange.

**Outer Eye**
Cut 2 yellow.

**Inner Eye**
Cut 2 black.

**Nose**
Cut 1 yellow.

**Mouth**
Cut 1 yellow.

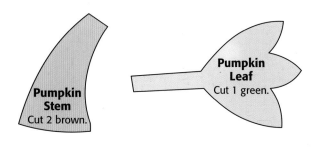

**Pumpkin Leaf**
Cut 1 green.

**Pumpkin Stem**
Cut 2 brown.

Enlarge pattern 150%.

BY SHEILA HAYNES RAUEN

# HALLOWEEN CAT AND PUMPKIN DOLLS

*This whimsical Halloween pair will add the spirit of Halloween to your home when perched on a mantel or buffet table in easy view. They were made using National Nonwoven's Wool Felt that was first prepared to have the look of boiled wool. This process does thicken the felt, making it more of a challenge to work with when creating smaller pieces. This should not be a problem for sewers with some experience. For the beginner, the projects can also be made using the felt without processing it.*

## MATERIALS

- National Nonwoven's Wool Felt (WCF001) in the following colors and yardages. (If you choose not to process the wool, you will need ⅛ yard less of black and dark orange.)
  - ⅝ yd. of Black
  - ⅜ yd. of Dark Orange
  - Scraps of Gold for cat's eyes and pumpkin's face
  - Scrap of Light Brown for pumpkin's stem
  - Scrap of Reets Relish (green) for leaf
  - Scrap of Smokey Marble (gray) for cat's nose
- Jacquard's White Neopaque paint for stamping
- 26-gauge yellow spool wire for whiskers
- 2 silver bugle beads for cat's fangs
- 4 pearl-white size 10 seed beads for highlights in eyes of cat and pumpkin
- Polyester fiberfill
- Access to a photocopier
- Patterns (pages 56–59)
- Pencil
- Scrap of Steam A Seam 2 (Warm & Natural) for facial details
- Tracing paper for overlay

- General sewing supplies: sewing machine, scissors, pins, and hand-sewing needle
- Black, gray, green, and orange sewing thread
- Dressmaker's tracing paper and dull pencil
- Lightweight tear-away stabilizer
- 1½" foam brush
- 1⅛" foam star stamp
- Wire cutters
- Fabric glue
- Halloween button, for hat (optional)

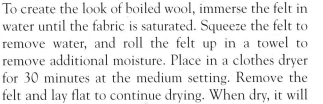

## ◆ PROCESSING WOOL ◆

To create the look of boiled wool, immerse the felt in water until the fabric is saturated. Squeeze the felt to remove water, and roll the felt up in a towel to remove additional moisture. Place in a clothes dryer for 30 minutes at the medium setting. Remove the felt and lay flat to continue drying. When dry, it will be ready to use.

After processing the felt, do not iron with steam because the fabric will return to its regular state. You may iron if necessary with a dry iron.

# INSTRUCTIONS

The detail stitching on this project was created using a sewing machine. Of course, you may do the buttonhole stitching (right) by hand if you prefer.

1. Photocopy the cat and pumpkin patterns on pages 56–59. From black felt, cut 2 cat head-body pieces, 2 tails, 4 upper and 4 lower legs, 1 gusset for the seat, and 1 star for the hat. From the orange felt, cut 2 pumpkins and 2 hat pieces. From the brown felt, cut 2 stems. From the green felt, cut 1 leaf with stem.

2. Trace the cat's eyes (on both the outside and inside lines) and nose, and the pumpkin's eyes, nose, and mouth in reverse onto the paper side of the Steam A Seam 2, leaving ¼" to ½" around the drawn areas. Cut around the shapes, leaving the allowance.

## TIP

To trace the pattern pieces in reverse, turn the pattern over and trace from the wrong side. If you cannot see the pattern well enough, darken the pattern lines with a black felt-tip pen or marker. Or, place the Steam A Seam 2 over the wrong side of the pattern and position on a sunlit window.

3. Following the manufacturer's instructions, remove the protective backing paper. Referring to the project photo for color placement, press each shape by hand onto the back of the appropriate color felt. Cut out the facial features on the drawn lines, and then remove the paper backing.

4. Trace the cat head-body piece and the pumpkin, including the faces, onto tracing paper. Place the cat tracing over the felt cat head-body piece and use as a guide for positioning the facial features. Fuse each shape into position, following the manufacturer's instructions and fusing the larger yellow eye pieces first, then fusing the black eye pieces on top. Repeat for the pumpkin.

5. Place 2 layers of lightweight tear-away stabilizer underneath the cat and pumpkin faces. Thread your sewing machine with black thread and outline the details on the faces with a machine

buttonhole stitch. Or use a hand buttonhole stitch, if you prefer.

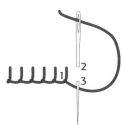

**Buttonhole Stitch**

6. Stitch the 2 stem pieces together using a straight stitch and black thread, using the stem pattern as a guide for the stitching lines. Also stitch the lines for the pumpkin's teeth, using the pattern as a guide.

7. Thread the machine with gray thread. Machine stitch lines in the cat's ears and chin using a straight stitch. I stitched mine using free-motion stitching by dropping the feed dogs and inserting a darning-embroidery foot.

8. Transfer the cat's mouth to the head-body piece, using the dressmaker's tracing paper and a pencil. Stitch over the marked line using a narrow machine satin stitch and gray thread.

9. Place 2 layers of tear-away stabilizer under the leaf and stitch the vein lines with a straight stitch and free-motion stitching, using the pattern as a guide.

10. Using the foam brush, apply a thin coat of white paint to the foam star stamp. Stamp stars onto the cat's head, body, legs, and tail pieces before constructing the cat. Refer to the project photo on page 52 for placement and reapply paint to the stamp before stamping each star. Allow stars to dry before proceeding.

11. Cut 3 pieces of yellow wire, 6" long. Push the wire through the felt from one side of the cat's muzzle to the other at the marked dots, so each wire will create 2 whiskers. After pushing all 3 wires into place with equal lengths of wire on each side of the muzzle, cut a piece of black felt approximately 1" by 1½" and glue it to the inside of the cat's face with fabric glue to stabilize the wires in place.

12. Wrap the ends of the wires 3 times around a pencil to coil. Whiskers will be adjusted again later when the cat is finished.

13. Referring to the pattern, sew 2 bugle beads below the cat's mouth line to create fangs. Sew pearl-white seed beads to cat's and pumpkin's eyes to give them sparkle.

14. Cut a slit in the pumpkin between the dots as shown on the pattern and, referring to the project photo on page 52, insert the stem and leaf into place. Sew along the slit using a satin stitch on your sewing machine.

15. Pin the pumpkin front and back pieces right sides together, folding the stem and leaf toward the center of the pumpkin. Sew the pieces together, leaving an opening on the side between the dots for turning. Turn the pumpkin right side out and stuff with polyester fiberfill. Slipstitch the opening closed.

16. Pin 2 matching leg pieces for the cat right sides together. Stitch, leaving an opening between the dots as indicated on the pattern. Turn right side out. Repeat for the remaining legs and the tail. The pieces will be stuffed later after they have all been sewn into place.

17. Pin the upper legs to the sides of the front head-body piece and lower legs along the lower edge of the front head-body piece within the seam line between the solid dots as indicated on the pattern; baste in place. Pin the tail between the open dots on the back head-body piece as indicated on the pattern; baste in place.

18. Pin the gusset to the lower edge of the cat front, right sides together with the cat's legs sandwiched in between. Sew between the gusset dots, backstitching at the ends.

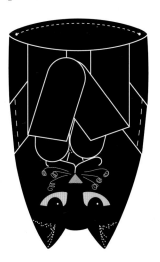

19. Place the front head-body piece right side up with the legs facing inward. Position the back head-body piece on top with the tail facing inward, and pin the front to the back. This will be more difficult if you are using felt that is thick from being processed, but it is worth the effort.

20. Stitch a continuous seam from the dot at the lower corner around the cat to the dot at the lower corner on the opposite side. Leave the seam open at the back along the gusset.

21. Trim seams, clip inside corners, and clip points on ears. Turn right side out. Stuff each leg with fiberfill and slipstitch the openings closed. Stuff the head and body of the cat and slipstitch the opening at the gusset and tail area closed. Stuff the tail last and slipstitch the opening closed.

22. Sew the 2 orange witch hat pieces together, leaving the bottom end open. Trim seams. Turn right side out.

23. Sew a black felt star or favorite Halloween button to the hat. Arrange whiskers as desired.

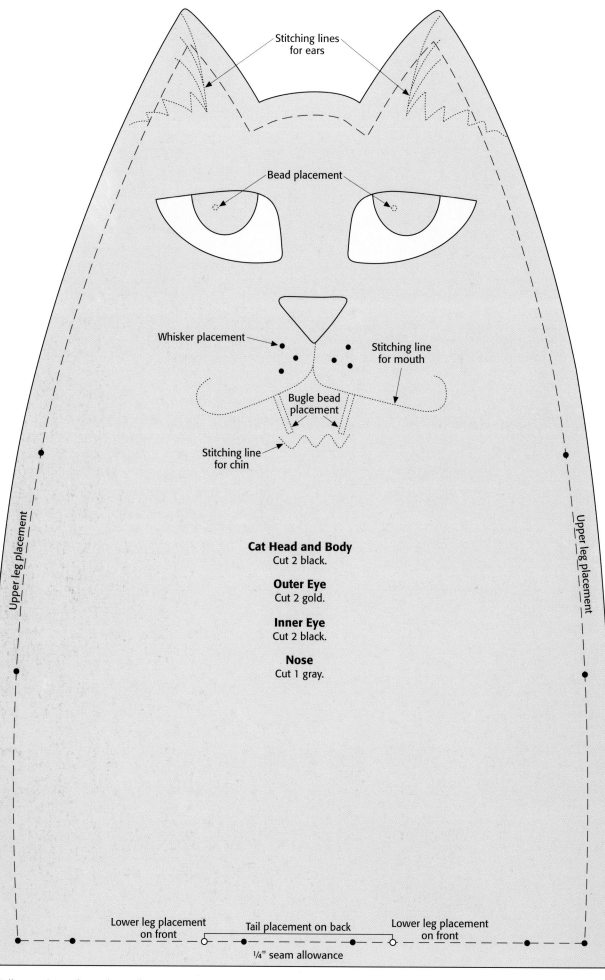

Stitching lines
for ears

Bead placement

Whisker placement

Stitching line
for mouth

Bugle bead
placement

Stitching line
for chin

Upper leg placement

Upper leg placement

**Cat Head and Body**
Cut 2 black.

**Outer Eye**
Cut 2 gold.

**Inner Eye**
Cut 2 black.

**Nose**
Cut 1 gray.

Lower leg placement
on front

Tail placement on back

Lower leg placement
on front

¼" seam allowance

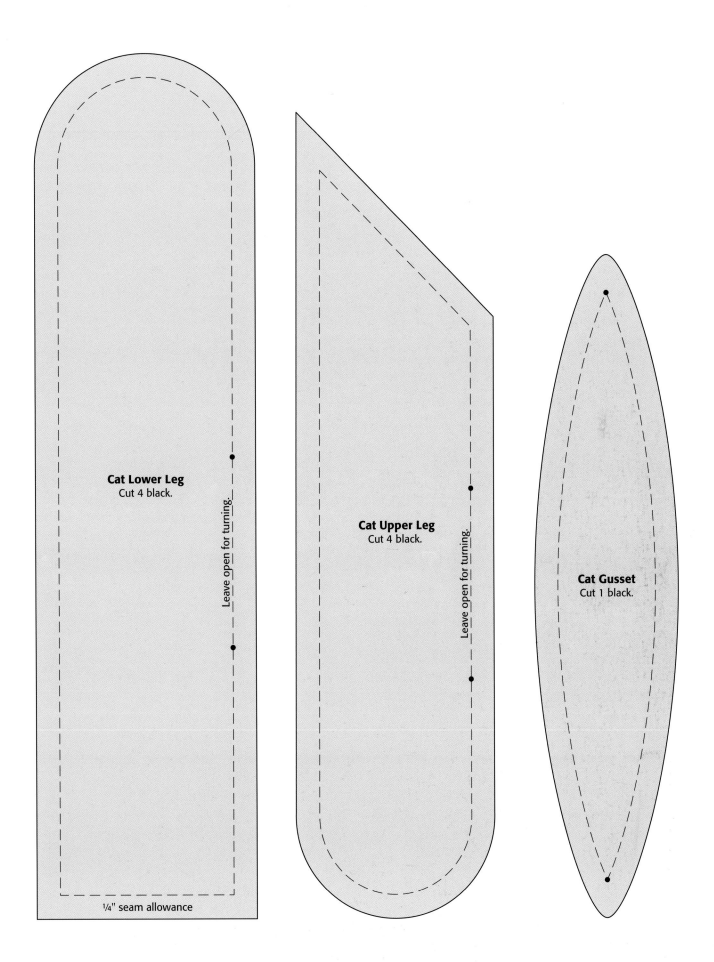

**Cat Lower Leg**
Cut 4 black.

Leave open for turning.

¼" seam allowance

**Cat Upper Leg**
Cut 4 black.

Leave open for turning.

**Cat Gusset**
Cut 1 black.

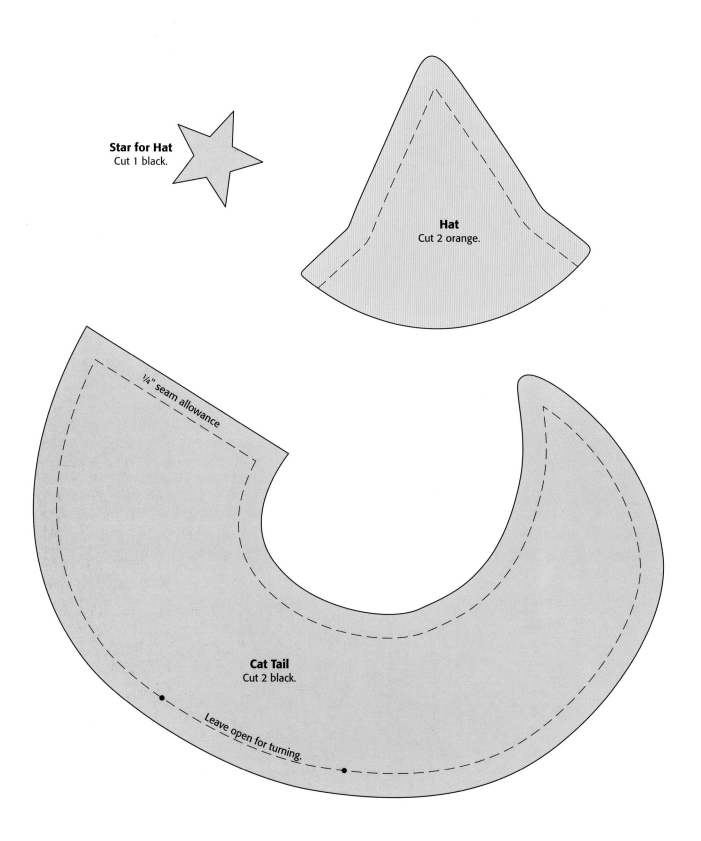

**Star for Hat**
Cut 1 black.

**Hat**
Cut 2 orange.

¼" seam allowance

**Cat Tail**
Cut 2 black.

Leave open for turning.

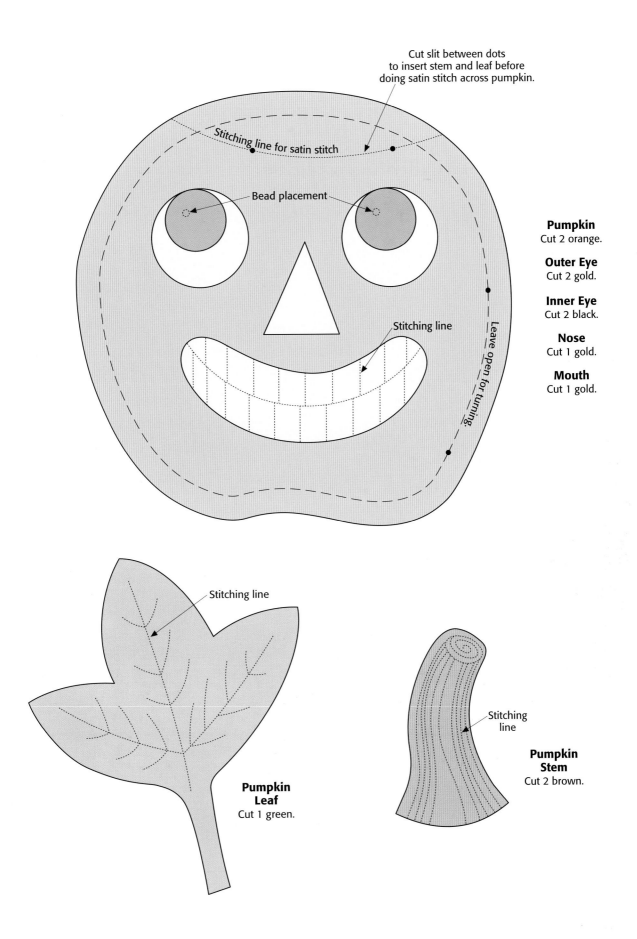

Cut slit between dots
to insert stem and leaf before
doing satin stitch across pumpkin.

Stitching line for satin stitch

Bead placement

**Pumpkin**
Cut 2 orange.

**Outer Eye**
Cut 2 gold.

**Inner Eye**
Cut 2 black.

**Nose**
Cut 1 gold.

**Mouth**
Cut 1 gold.

Stitching line

Leave open for turning.

Stitching line

**Pumpkin
Leaf**
Cut 1 green.

Stitching
line

**Pumpkin
Stem**
Cut 2 brown.

BY DAWN ANDERSON

# BEADED CANDLE WREATH AND BAT MEDALLION

Turn a pillar candle into a decorative Halloween accessory with a gnarled candle wreath of orange and gray glass beads and a bat medallion accent. The beads are strung on lengths of wire to resemble vines, which are then intertwined to make a small wreath. The bat medallion is simply a sealing-wax wafer, ordinarily used for sealing an envelope. It was heated and then sprinkled with embossing powder to match the beads, heated again, and embedded with a bat charm while still warm.

Another festive Halloween project you might want to try are the organza favor bags shown at left. Make up one for each of your guests and fill with your favorite Halloween candy. You'll find the instructions on page 64.

## CANDLE WREATH

### MATERIALS

- 3" x 6" pillar candle and desired candle holder
- Size 11/0 Rocaille seed beads:
    - 1 hank (10 strings) of silver-lined gray
    - 1 hank (10 strings) of silver-lined orange
- 6" vial of size 6/0 silver-lined orange seed beads
- Assorted accent beads:
    - 36 smoky orange 6 mm beads
    - 18 orange 6 mm beads
    - 16 orange 11 mm x 7 mm leaf beads (with hole running from base to tip)
- 28-gauge silver spool wire
- Wire cutters
- Round-nose pliers

### ◆ ◆ ◆ ◆ TIP ◆ ◆ ◆ ◆

You can easily adjust the size of the candle wreath to fit other sizes of pillar candles and candle holders. To adjust the lengths of your beaded strands for a custom fit, measure the distance around the outside of your candle (the circumference) and add 3" to obtain your first measurement. Measure the circumference of your candle holder and use this measurement for your second measurement. Bead as many strands as necessary to obtain the fullness of the wreath shown in the photo, varying the lengths of the beaded strands between the two measurements.

# INSTRUCTIONS

1. Cut nine 40" lengths of wire using wire cutters. Loop wire several times around the round-nose pliers, about 3" from one end of the wire, to create a stop point for the beads. Randomly thread both gray and orange size 11/0 seed beads onto the wire, pushing beads down to the stop point. Start by threading about 2" of beads onto the wire, threading a size 6/0 orange seed bead onto the wire occasionally.

2. Slide an accent bead onto the wire, stopping about 1¼" to 2" from the last bead. To secure, bend the wire back on itself and twist in a tight spiral until the wire is twisted all the way back to the main strand.

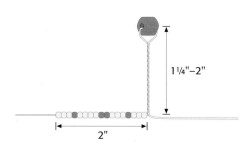

3. Resume bead stringing, adding an accent bead on a twisted wire stem approximately every 1⅛" to 1⅜". Occasionally substitute a size 6/0 seed bead for an accent bead. You can also add a cluster of size 6/0 seed beads instead of an accent bead. To do this, thread a size 6/0 seed bead onto the wire, stopping about 1½" from the last bead. Bend the wire back on itself and twist in a tight spiral for about ⅜". Add another size 6/0 seed bead about ⅝" from the end of the twisted wire. Bend the wire back on itself and twist in a tight spiral for about ⅜", and then add another size 6/0 seed bead about ⅜" from the end of the twisted wire in the same manner. Continue twisting until wire is twisted all the way back to the main beaded strand. This will give you 1 twisted stem with a cluster of 3 branching beads at the end.

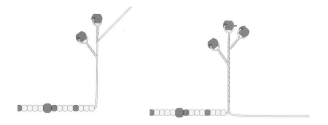

4. To add leaf accent beads, thread a leaf bead onto the wire, stopping about 1¼" to 2" from the last bead. Add a size 11/0 orange seed bead and insert wire back through the leaf bead, pulling snug. Add another size 11/0 orange seed bead to trap the leaf bead in place. Hold the wires together and twist in a tight spiral all the way back to the main strand.

5. Bead a total of 9 bead strands, varying the lengths between 12¾" and 13½". Leave about 2" at the end of each strand without any accent beads. Take one strand and uncoil the wire at the stop point. Insert the end of the wire into the beads at the beginning of the strand, likewise inserting the beginning wire into the end of the strand for about ¾" on each side to make a complete circle. Pull wire tails out and add an accent bead to each, stopping about 1½" from the main strand. For each, bend wire back on itself and twist in a tight spiral until the wire is twisted all the way back to the main beaded strand. Insert wire ends into the holes of 5 continuous beads along the main strand and clip close to the exit point as shown.

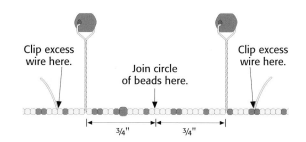

6. Wrap another beaded strand around the first circle of beads, wrapping about 3 times to give the look of intertwined vines. Join the ends as for the first strand of beads. Repeat with the remaining 7 strands of beads to make a beaded, wreath-like candle collar.

# BAT MEDALLION

## MATERIALS

- Sealing-wax wafer
- Pearluster embossing powder in Pearlized Carnelian (Stampendous!)
- Bat charm
- Wire cutters
- Jewelry file
- Newsprint
- Two 8½" x 11" sheets of scrap paper
- Heat embossing tool
- Tin can approximately the same diameter as pillar candle from candle wreath instructions
- Tape
- Lighter
- Taper candle

## INSTRUCTIONS

1. Using wire cutters, clip the hanger from the bat charm. File rough edges with a jewelry file. Set charm aside.

### TIP

When clipping the hanger off, point the hanger end away from you toward the ground so that the piece being cut off falls to the floor instead of flying up at you.

2. Cover the work surface with newsprint. Place a sheet of scrap paper on the newsprint. Set the sealing-wax wafer in the center of the paper. Using the heat embossing tool, apply heat until the surface of the wax wafer is melted. Immediately sprinkle with embossing powder, shaking excess powder off onto the second sheet of scrap paper. Again using the heat embossing tool, heat the embossing powder until melted, and immediately set the charm into the embossed wafer. Do not press in too far, because the charm will continue to sink into the wafer as it cools. Quickly wrap the paper with the wafer around the tin can to shape the wafer while still warm. Tape the paper in place, place the can on its side with the wafer up, and allow the wafer to cool.

3. Place the pillar candle on its side. Remove the cooled wafer from the paper. Light the taper candle and drip about 3 drops of wax onto the pillar candle, between one-third and one-half of the way down from the top of the candle. Immediately set the sealing-wax wafer with the charm onto the melted wax to secure it to the candle. Allow to cool.

### TIP

Because the embossing powder creates a barrier between the charm and the sealing wax, the charm may come loose. If it becomes dislodged from the wafer, simply secure it back into position with a bit of clear-drying tacky glue.

4. Set the beaded candle wreath on your desired candle holder and set the candle into the wreath. Arrange beaded vines around the collar as desired.

# ORGANZA FAVOR BAGS

## MATERIALS *(for 10 bags)*

- ½ yd. of orange organza fabric
- Orange thread to match fabric
- 4¼ yds. of narrow metallic ribbon
- Candy
- Sewing equipment and supplies: sewing machine, iron and ironing board, rotary cutter, ruler, self-healing cutting mat, sewing shears, and pins

## INSTRUCTIONS *(for 1 bag)*

1. Cut a 4" x 13¼" rectangle from fabric. Fold rectangle in half lengthwise, wrong sides together. Stitch ⅜" from each long side. Trim seam allowances to ⅛". Turn bag right sides together and press seams flat. Stitch ¼" from previous seam lines to make French seams. Turn right side out and press.

2. Fold the upper edge of the bag down ¼" toward the inside and press, than fold another ¼" and press again. Stitch close to the first fold. Stitch slowly, stopping as necessary with the needle down to reposition the bag.

3. Fill the bag with candy and tie a 15" length of ribbon about 1½" from the bag opening.

BY JILL MACKAY

# MOSAIC PUMPKIN LANTERN

*This glass mosaic pumpkin lantern allows the flickering candlelight to dance and glow, adding warmth and color to your Halloween festivities. The sizes of stained glass pieces listed in the materials list are the actual amounts of glass used in this project. However, you will not be able to purchase these sizes from a store. Most stained glass comes in 12" x 12" or larger pieces. The stained glass used was mainly translucent with swirls of opaque mixed in. You do not want to use straight opaque because it will not let as much candlelight through. Four different kinds of clear textured glass were used on this lantern. Though this takes more diligence to clean after grouting, it has a much richer feel due to the textures themselves. The textures also play with the light, reflecting it in a more jewel-like fashion than plain clear glass would.*

## MATERIALS

- Lantern with 4¾" x 6" glass panes
- 9" x 12" piece of orange stained glass for pumpkin
- 3" x 12" piece of gold stained glass for facial details
- 3" x 12" piece of light green stained glass for pumpkin stems
- 4" x 4" piece of dark green stained glass for stem ends
- Four 3" x 12" pieces of clear textured glass in assorted textures
- 4-oz. tube of clear silicone adhesive
- 1 lb. of black sanded grout
- Access to a photocopy machine
- Patterns (pages 68–71)
- Scissors
- Glass cleaner

- Paper towels
- Masking tape, 1" wide
- Black permanent marker
- Gallery Glasses or safety glasses (Plaid)
- Mosaic glass cutters (Plaid)
- 6 paper plates
- Old towel
- Craft sticks
- Plastic drop cloth
- 2 plastic buckets or containers
- Dust mask
- Old measuring cup
- Rubber gloves
- Wooden spoon
- Sponge
- Soft polishing cloth (not terry cloth)
- Toothpicks

- Always wear safety goggles while cutting or nipping glass.

- Before you glue a shard of glass in place on one of the black lines of the pattern, you'll want to remove that portion of the black line. Clean away only the portion of the line that will be covered by the piece of glass you are gluing. If you do not remove the pattern lines these black lines will be visible through the stained glass. To remove the marker line, wipe with a paper towel dampened with glass cleaner.

- When gluing, you can spread the glue around on the surface of the glass panel with the tip of the tube or by putting the glue on the back of each shard of glass. Either way, make sure there is enough glue to adhere the piece of stained glass securely to the surface of the panel but not so much that when you press it firmly in place the glue squishes up and fills the spaces between pieces. The spaces between the pieces are necessary to hold the grout. Use a craft stick to clear away any extra glue that might seep into these spaces. The spaces between pieces should be approximately 1/16" wide or slightly larger and should be kept consistent in width.

## INSTRUCTIONS

1. Photocopy the 4 patterns on pages 68–71. Cut out the pumpkin shapes with scissors, removing the eyes, nose, and mouth.

2. Clean the glass panes on the lantern with glass cleaner and paper towels. Tape a pumpkin pattern to each side of the lantern, aligning the corner of each pattern with 1 corner of each glass pane. Trace around all 4 patterns using a permanent marker.

3. Put on safety glasses. Using the mosaic cutters, nip all the glass except the dark green into smaller, odd-shaped pieces (shards) in a variety of sizes. Keep the different colors separate, each on its own paper plate.

4. Lay the lantern on its side on a towel. Glue orange glass shards inside the pumpkin outline, nipping and shaping the shards with the mosaic cutters to create the desired fit of pieces.

5. For the eyes and nose (and the mouth on one of the pumpkin designs), glue small gold glass shards into place, shaping the shards as necessary with the mosaic cutters.

6. Glue light green glass shards to the stem section, shaping the shards as necessary with the mosaic cutters. Following the pattern and using the mosaic cutters, shape a piece of dark green glass to fit the stem end.

7. Glue clear glass of different textures to the background area, shaping the glass as necessary to fit the space.

8. Repeat steps 4 through 7 to cover the remaining 3 sides of the lantern with glass shards. Let dry overnight.

9. Cover your work space with the drop cloth in preparation for grouting. Fill 1 bucket with water.

10. Carefully mask off the entire frame of the lantern on the exterior only. Place the edge of the masking tape right up next to the glass panels but not extending past the edge of the frame.

11. Put on the dust mask and rubber gloves, and pour approximately 6 oz. of grout into the second plastic container. Following manufacturer's instructions, mix the grout thoroughly with gloved fingers. Apply grout over the entire surface of the first panel, using your gloved fingertips to push grout down into the crevices. Carefully fill all the spaces and make sure grout fills the outside edges as well. Use your fingertip to carefully smooth these grout lines. Repeat the grouting process on the remaining 3 lantern panels.

12. Wet the sponge in water, wringing out the excess. Sponge away the excess grout, starting with the first panel. Be careful not to remove too much grout, or your glass shards will not stay in place. You might need to go back and fill the grout lines around the outside edges again if small amounts of grout become dislodged by the sponge. Let dry for 15 to 20 minutes, and then carefully remove the masking tape. Polish clean using a soft cloth. You will need to use a toothpick to remove the grout that has become caught in the grooves and dips of the textured glass. Be meticulous, clean thoroughly, and then polish one last time with the soft cloth.

Side 1

Side 2

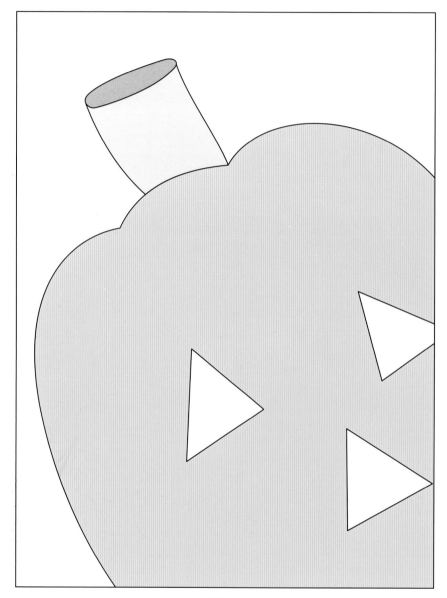

Side 3

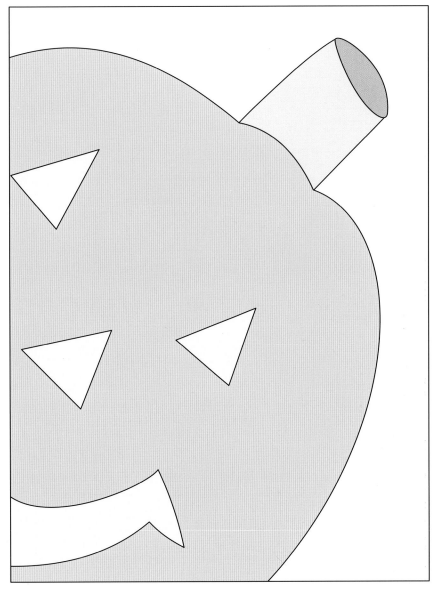

Side 4

BY MICHAEL BALL

# PAINTED WITCH AND BAT LANTERNS

*The eerie designs on these Halloween lanterns look complex but are really quite simple to create. The glass panes are first painted with a background of two similar colors, and then the outlines of the Halloween images are transferred on top and filled in with black paint. The glass panes in these lanterns measure 3" x 3¾", but you can enlarge or reduce the patterns as necessary to fit any rectangular piece of glass.*

## MATERIALS *(for 2 lanterns)*

- 2 lanterns with rectangular glass panels (Panels in this project measure 3" x 3¾".)
- Black contour paste
- Glass paints in the following colors: deep blue, turquoise, clear, white, black, orange, and yellow
- Water for water-based paint or compatible solvent for oil-based paint
- Access to a photocopy machine
- Patterns (page 75)
- Double-stick tape
- Newsprint
- Mixing palette or ice-cube tray
- Toothpicks
- Paintbrushes (Loew-Cornell):
  - Two of the La Corneille Golden Taklon Series 7000, #5 round
  - One of the La Corneille Golden Taklon Series 7500, #10/0 filbert
- Fine-tip black overhead-projector pen

## WITCH LANTERN

## INSTRUCTIONS

1. Photocopy the pattern on page 75, enlarging or reducing as necessary so that the design fits neatly within 1 glass pane of your lantern, allowing a bit of extra space all around the border for outlining. Trim the pattern to fit inside the lantern. Use a piece of double-stick tape to secure the template to the back of a pane of glass, inside the lantern.

2. Cover your work surface with newsprint. Use black contour paste to trace the outline around the witch panel design (not around the witch herself). Allow to dry for 2 hours.

3. Lay the lantern down with the panel you are working on facing upward. Use black glass paint to fill in the areas between the contour paste and the edge of the glass panel. Allow to dry, following the manufacturer's instructions.

4. Pour about 2 teaspoons of deep blue glass paint onto a mixing palette. An old ice-cube tray makes an ideal mixing palette for glass paint. If you are using a water-based paint, add 1 drop of water; if you are using an oil-based paint, add a drop of the appropriate solvent. Add about 1 teaspoon of clear glass paint and 1 drop of white paint. The addition of this small quantity of white paint adds a misty semi-opaque quality. Stir the paint thoroughly with a toothpick. Don't be tempted to stir with your brush as this can easily introduce bubbles of air into the paint that might be hard to remove. Mix up some turquoise paint in the same way, adding water or solvent, clear paint, and a small amount of white paint.

5. Working quickly, apply a wash of the deep blue mixture over the upper half of the panel with a round brush, starting from the top and working down, moving the brush from side to side in smooth horizontal strokes. Pick up your second round brush and use it to apply a wash of the turquoise over the lower half of the panel, work-ing from the bottom up. Brush from side to side over the area where the 2 colors join to create a subtle gradation.

6. The drying time of the paint will depend upon the room temperature. Allow the paint to set for 15 minutes, and then use a toothpick to make a line in the paint inside the outline of the moon. If the paint flows back into the line that you created, leave the paint for an additional 15 minutes; then repeat. Continue in this manner, if necessary, until the paint does not flow back into the scratched area. Scratch away the outline of the moon, and scratch off dots randomly over the design, outside the witch outline, for the stars. Allow the paint to dry overnight.

7. Using the pattern as a guide, draw the outline of the witch using the fine-tip black pen. Fill in the outline with black glass paint using the filbert brush and allow to dry, following the manufac-turer's instructions. Remove the pattern.

 ## BAT LANTERN

## INSTRUCTIONS

1. Follow steps 1 to 3 in the instructions for making the witch lantern. Pour about 2 teaspoons of yel-low glass paint onto a mixing palette. If you are using a water-based paint, add 1 drop of water; if you are using an oil-based paint, add a drop of the appropriate solvent. Add about 1 teaspoon of clear glass paint and 1 drop of white paint. Stir the paint thoroughly with a toothpick. Don't be tempted to stir with your brush as this can easily introduce bubbles of air into the paint that might be hard to remove. Mix up some orange paint in the same way, adding water or solvent, clear paint, and a small amount of white paint.

2. Working quickly, apply a wash of the yellow mix-ture over the upper half of the panel with a round brush, starting from the top and working down, moving the brush from side to side in smooth strokes. Pick up your second brush and use it to apply a wash of the orange over the lower half of the panel, working from the bottom up. Brush from side to side in a slight arcing fashion over the area where the two colors join to create a subtle gradation (see the project photo on page 72). Continue painting up to and around the dashed moon outline. The distinction between the moon and sky should be subtle. If it is too harsh, pick up your yellow brush and blend some more yellow back into the orange. Allow the paint to dry overnight; the exact drying time will depend upon the room temperature.

3. Using the pattern as a guide, draw the outline of the bats using the fine-tip black pen. Fill in the outline with black glass paint using the filbert brush and allow to dry, following the manufac-turer's instructions. Remove the pattern.

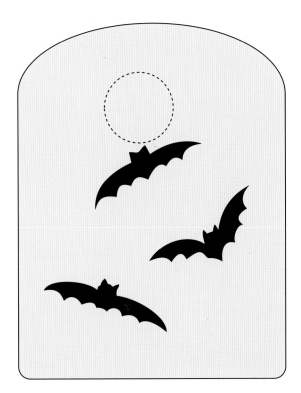

BY GENEVIEVE A. STERBENZ

# BEADED SPIDERWEB AND SPIDERS

*Shimmering candlelight, illuminates the sparkling silver of a beaded spiderweb that appears to be dripping in dew, with rhinestone spiders still busy at work. Decorate your windowsills or mantel table with this new take on these creepy critters.*

*I found the best way to create the beaded spiderweb was to work within a wooden picture frame. I hammered nails around the frame and used them to anchor the strands of the web. The ornate spiders are simply made from a few beads and a rhinestone button with a shank. The shank is important because it acts as an anchor for the head wire and beaded leg wires that are added. Search local craft stores for interesting buttons and beads. You may want to explore thrift stores or flea markets, as well.*

 SPIDERWEB

## MATERIALS

- 11" x 14" wooden picture frame
- 24-gauge spool wire in silver
- 2 hanks (10 strings each) of silver-lined clear Rocaille seed beads
- Twelve 9 mm x 6 mm crystal drop beads
- Access to photocopier
- Pattern (page 81)
- Hammer
- Nails
- Ruler
- Wire cutters
- Needle-nose pliers
- Scrap of heavy cotton or flannel fabric

# INSTRUCTIONS

1. Separate the glass and backing from the picture frame. Set all but the frame aside. Photocopy the pattern on page 81, enlarging by 225% and reversing the image. Place the frame, wrong side up, on your work surface. Align the pattern on the back of the frame and use a hammer to tap in nails where the legs of the spider web meet the frame.

2. Unwind about 15" of wire from spool but do not cut the wire. Take a rough measurement by placing one end of the wire at the nail in position A, and stretch the wire diagonally to the opposite nail also in position A, as the pattern indicates. Add 2" extra and cut the wire. Use pliers to crimp one end of the cut wire. Lay the scrap of heavy cotton or flannel on a clean, flat workspace to prevent stray beads from rolling away. Separate 1 string of seed beads from the hank and lay on the flannel. Without letting the beads fall off the string, insert the uncrimped end of the cut wire into the center of the beads, 1" at a time, pulling them off the string until all but 2" of wire is strung with beads. Crimp the end of the wire using pliers.

3. Transfer the beaded wire to the frame, wrapping 1" of wire at the end of the beaded wire around a nail in position A. Stretch beaded wire taut to the remaining A nail. Push beads away from the end and wrap 1" of wire around the nail. Repeat steps 2 and 3 to add beaded wire to nail positions B and C. When applying beaded wires across the center of the web, push beads aside and overlay the wires.

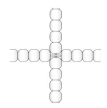

The center of the web will get crowded with beads, so wires can be moved slightly off center. Add half strands D, E, F, and G last, using pliers to twist one end around the nail and the opposite end around one of the interior wires. Trim off excess wire.

4. Unwind about 20" of wire from the spool and cut with wire cutters. String the wire with seed beads as explained in step 2. Twist one end of beaded wire to one beaded support wire already attached to the frame, 1" away from the center as the pattern indicates. Pull the beaded wire taut and toward the second support wire in a counterclockwise direction. Weave beaded wire underneath the support wire and then back over it and under again towards the next support wire, moving beads aside so the wires lie flat. Continue moving the beaded wire in this manner, following the pattern until the wire comes back to the starting point. At the end, wrap wire around the beaded support wire; twist and clip the excess. Repeat this step for subsequent rows of beads to increase the web size, using the pattern as a guide. Note: Not all rows make a complete circle back to the starting point.

5. Snip twelve 1" lengths of wire. String 1 piece through the hole in each crystal drop bead and make a loop at the end to secure. Twist the exposed end of wire around beaded wire on the web as indicated by the dots on the pattern, or in a different position if you so desire.

# SPIDERS

## MATERIALS

### For 1 gold spider:

- 24-gauge gold spool wire
- 1 hank (10 strings) of size 10/0 gold Rocaille seed beads
- 13 mm x 6 mm oval copper bead
- 1" or ⅝" amber rhinestone button with shank

### For 1 black spider:

- 24-gauge silver spool wire
- 1 hank (10 strings) of size 10/0 black Rocaille seed beads
- 13 mm x 6 mm diamond-shaped black bead
- ⅝" black rhinestone button with shank

### For both spiders:

- Ruler
- Wire cutters
- Scrap of heavy cotton or flannel fabric
- Needle-nose pliers

## INSTRUCTIONS *(for 1 spider)*

1. Cut a 6" length of wire using wire cutters. Slide 1 seed bead onto the wire. Bring the bead to the midpoint and bend the wire in half. Slide the oval or diamond bead onto both wires. String a second seed bead onto one wire and push up to oval or diamond bead. Twist wires together at the base of the seed bead to secure. Then thread the wires through the shank of the rhinestone button. Bring the ends of the wire back up and over the shank, and thread wires through the shank again. Pull taut to secure in place.

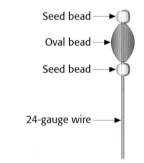

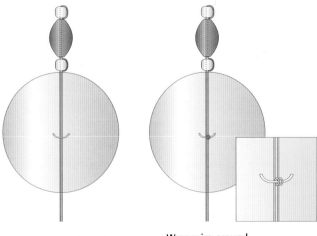

Thread wires through button shank.

Wrap wire around shank and back down.

2. Unwind wire from spool and cut 4 pieces, 7½" long, using wire cutters. Place the body of the spider belly side up. Take 1 wire and thread the end underneath the center body wire, back over the top, and underneath the center wire again. Add the remaining 3 legs at different points down the center wire as shown.

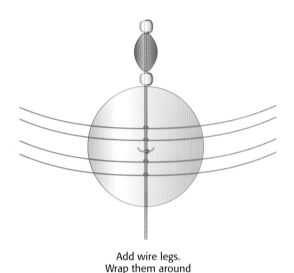

Add wire legs.
Wrap them around
center wire stem.

3. Lay the scrap of heavy cotton or flannel under the spider, belly side up, to prevent stray beads from rolling away. Lay a hank of seed beads next to the spider. Separate 1 string of beads from the hank. Without letting the beads fall off the string, carefully move the strand to 1 leg and insert the end of the wire into the holes of the beads, letting beads slide off the string and onto the wire. Leave ¼" of wire at the end of the leg. Wrap end around wire at the top of the last bead; trim excess with wire cutters. Repeat on the opposite side of the leg. Continue beading the remaining 3 pieces of wire on both the right and left sides. Bend legs at their midpoint as desired.

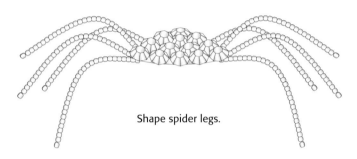

Shape spider legs.

4. Secure spiders to the web at desired locations by wrapping a 2" length of spool wire through the shank of the rhinestone button and around the web, twisting to secure. Trim excess wire.

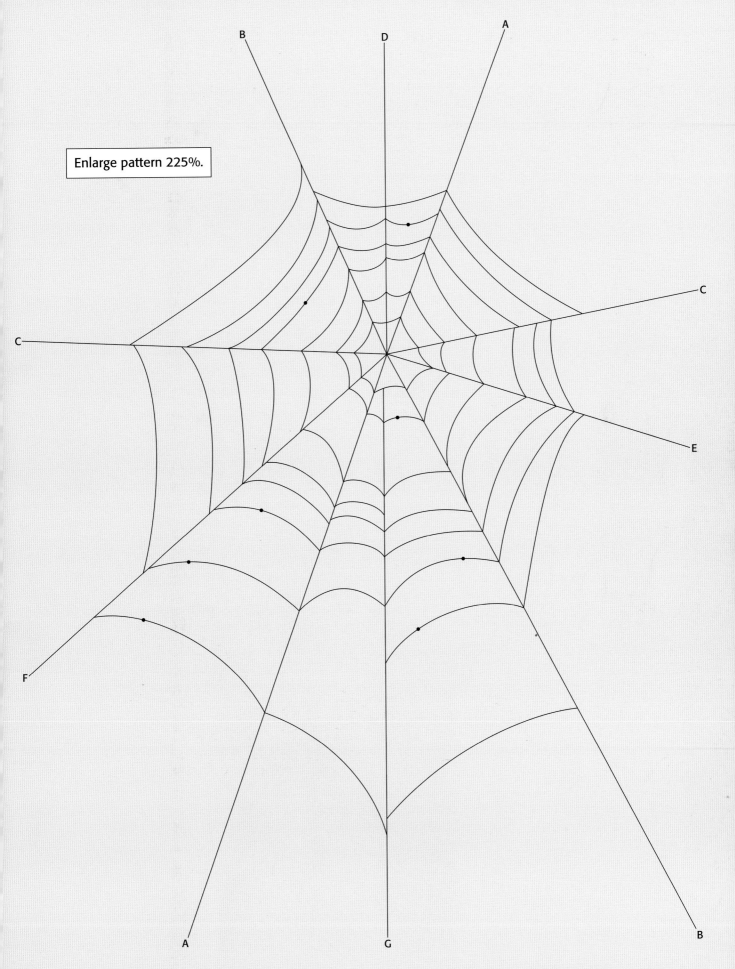

Enlarge pattern 225%.

By Jennifer Ferguson

# STENCILED SKELETON BANNER

*Enjoy the spirit of Halloween with this festive banner featuring a dancing skeleton figure topped with a pumpkin head. The skeleton pattern can be found on page 85. The stenciled checkerboard was created with a ready-made border stencil.*

## MATERIALS

- Cambric cloth or any paintable canvas
- Americana Acrylic Paints in the following colors: Light Buttermilk, Black, Violet Haze, Canyon Orange, White, Burnt Orange, Taffy Cream, Hauser Light Green, Plantation Pine, and Moon Yellow
- Rotary cutter, clear acrylic grid ruler, and self-healing cutting mat
- Foam roller
- Removable painter's tape
- 2⅜"-wide checkerboard border stencil with ¾" checks
- Stencil brushes
- Paper towels
- Foam applicator
- Palette
- Access to a photocopier
- Pattern (page 85)
- Template plastic
- Pen
- X-Acto knife
- Burnisher, such as a blunt wooden tool
- ⅜" x 36" wood dowel, cut to 26¼" long
- Two acorn dowel caps
- Wood glue
- Pencil
- Double-stick carpet tape

## ◆ STENCILING BASICS ◆

**Loading the brush.** Pour a small amount of paint onto your paint palette and dip brush into the paint. Work the paint into the bristles by rubbing in a circular motion on a clean area of the palette. Hold the brush upright and rub excess paint onto a folded paper towel; then wipe the brush across the paper towel in an X motion to remove excess paint.

**Applying the paint.** Hold the brush upright and apply the paint by swirling the brush around in a circular motion onto the canvas.

**Shading.** To add more than a single paint color to a given area, creating shading and depth, allow the first layer of paint to dry completely. Then, using a new brush, apply the second color.

## INSTRUCTIONS

1. Cut the cambric cloth or canvas to 25" x 37" using a rotary cutter, ruler, and cutting mat. Paint the complete canvas Light Buttermilk, using the foam roller. You'll need to apply several coats to create opaque, even coverage. Allow paint to dry between coats.

2. Tape off an area measuring 15" x 24¾" in the middle of the canvas, leaving 5" borders on the sides and bottom and a 7¼" border at the top. Test-fit your checkerboard stencil around the outside of the taped area to be sure the checkerboard design fits evenly and is in alignment at

Color Plan

corners. You want about ⅛" of space between the inner tape edge and the checkerboard border. Adjust the size of the taped-off area if necessary. Burnish the edges of the tape to prevent seepage of paint. Tape off a 2½"-wide outer border on the sides and bottom of the canvas and a 4¾"-wide border at the top. Again, check to be sure your checkerboard design fits evenly between the taped off center area and the taped off outer border. Paint the 15" x 24¾" area in the middle of the canvas and the outer border with Black. Again, this may take several coats to create opaque, even coverage. Remove the tape.

3. Tape the checkerboard stencil to the Light Buttermilk border. Stencil ¾" checks (a triple row), starting with Violet Haze checks first. Remove and reposition the stencil as necessary to stencil the entire border. Clean the stencil, reposition on the border, and stencil remaining checks with Canyon Orange.

4. Tape off a ¼" border, 1" inside the checkerboard design. Burnish the edges of the tape and paint the ¼" border with Violet Haze, using a foam applicator.

5. Photocopy the skeleton pattern on page 85, enlarging by 200%. Transfer the design to template plastic with a pen. Cut out the design on the marked lines, using an X-Acto knife and cutting mat, except do not cut out the stem or facial details on the pumpkin. Make 2 additional stencils slightly larger than the pumpkin head. Draw in the pumpkin head and all the facial details and the stem on both. On 1 stencil, cut out only the yellow eyes, nose, mouth, and stem, and on the other cut out only the black eye centers. Use the remaining lines as a guide for aligning the stencils.

6. Center the main stencil on the canvas and tape in place. Referring to "Stenciling Basics" on page 83, stencil the stars, skeleton bones, and pumpkin head White and allow the paint to dry. Then stencil the pumpkin head again with Canyon Orange and add shading around the outer edges with Burnt Orange.

7. Stencil the moon with Taffy Cream and the bats with Violet Haze. Remove the stencil.

8. Position and tape the stencil with the facial details over the pumpkin, aligning the edges. Stencil the stem with Hauser Light Green and add shading with Plantation Pine. Stencil the eyes, nose, and mouth with Taffy Cream and add shading with Moon Yellow. Remove the stencil.

9. Position and tape the eye stencil over the pumpkin. Stencil the eye centers with Black. Remove the stencil.

10. Paint the wood dowel and acorn dowel caps with the foam applicator and black paint. Allow to dry. Glue caps to ends of dowel and allow to dry.

11. Measuring 2½" above the top checkerboard border, make a pencil mark on the underside of both the right and left edges of the banner. Place the banner face down on your work surface. Lay the dowel on the banner, aligning with pencil marks. Fold the excess canvas over the dowel, securing in place on the back with double-stick carpet tape.

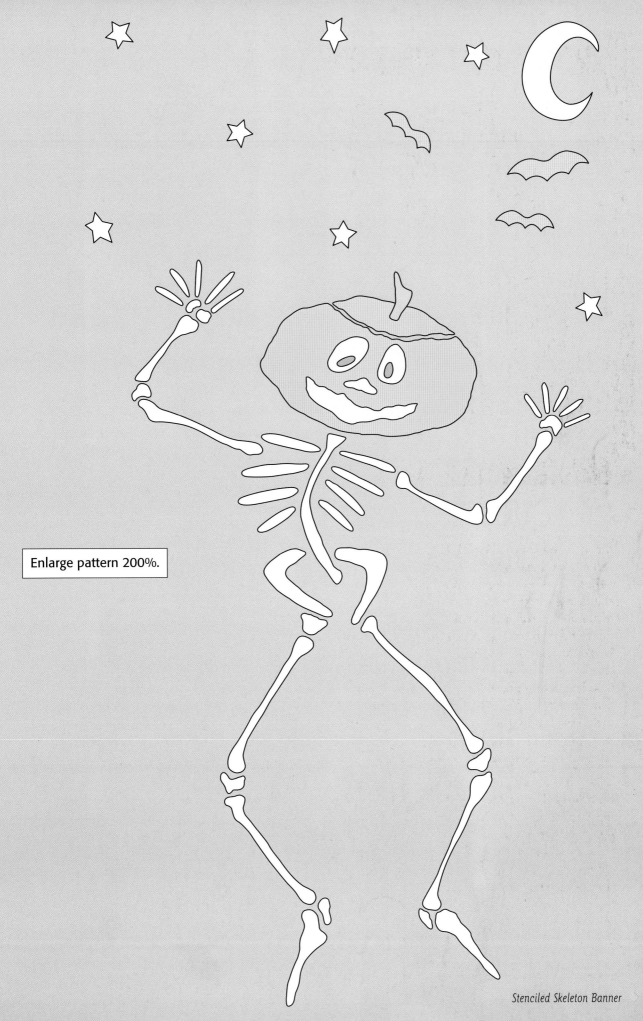

Enlarge pattern 200%.

BY DAWN ANDERSON

# GLITTERED PUMPKIN BASKET

*Use this sparkling pumpkin to hold a basketful of wrapped Halloween candies. The basket is made from a carveable artificial pumpkin that was first painted, and then covered with glue and sprinkled with ultra-fine and micro glitters. The facial details were recessed slightly by carving away the outer skin of the pumpkin before painting and glittering. The glittered portion of the handle consists of a wooden tassel head glued to each side of a round wooden bead. The ensemble is painted and glittered to match the basket and then placed onto the wire handle. The handle is more decorative than functional. Although the handle can support the weight of the basket, it may not be sturdy enough to use when the basket is weighted with heavy treats.*

## MATERIALS

- Newsprint
- 10" carveable pumpkin
- Gesso
- Orange tissue paper
- Four 8½" x 11" sheets of orange mulberry paper
- Americana Acrylic Paints in the following colors: Tangerine, White Wash, French Vanilla, Cadmium Orange, and Lamp Black
- Glitter (Barbara Trombley's Original Art Glittering System) in the following colors: Ultra Fine Tangerine, Microfine Poupon, Ultra Fine Florida Orange, and Ultra Fine Black
- Glamour Dust (DecoArt)
- Pencil
- Vinyl measuring tape
- Mat knife
- Access to photocopy machine
- Pattern (page 89)
- Scissors
- Masking tape
- X-Acto knife
- Design Paste (Aleene's 3D Accents)
- Mod Podge
- Painter's gloves
- Paintbrushes (Loew-Cornell):
  - La Corneille Golden Taklon Series 7300 #20 and #0 shaders
  - La Corneille Golden Taklon Series 7500 ¼" angular shader
  - La Corneille Golden Taklon Series 7500 #10/0 filbert
- Old ⅜" and 1" stiff-bristled brushes (for glue)
- Incredibly Tacky glue (api's Crafter's Pick)
- Four 8½" x 11" sheets of scrap paper (for glittering)
- Dust mask
- Awl
- Toothpick
- Four ⅛" orange eyelets
- 22-gauge black copper spool wire
- 36" of 16-gauge black copper wire
- ⅞" wooden bead
- Two ⅝" x 1¼" wooden tassel heads

- Round-nose pliers
- Sand-N-Stain Wood Glue (api's Crafter's Pick)
- Wire cutters
- Two ½" diameter orange buttons with 2 holes each
- Scrap of orange felt

# INSTRUCTIONS

1. Cover a work surface with newsprint. Using a pencil, draw a line around the carveable pumpkin about 3¼" to 3½" down from the stem (distance may vary due to the shape of your pumpkin). Strive for an even line all the way around the pumpkin. Cut on the marked line with the mat knife and remove the top of the pumpkin.

2. Photocopy or trace the pumpkin face pattern on page 89. Cut on the outer marked lines. Tape the eyes, nose, and mouth to the pumpkin with masking tape, centering between the top and bottom of the pumpkin. Trace around the facial features with a pencil, and then remove pattern pieces.

3. Using an X-Acto knife, cut on the marked lines about ⅛" deep, and slice away the outer shell of the pumpkin within the facial features. Strive to keep the surface as smooth and even as possible, about a scant ⅛" deep. It will be somewhat jagged and lumpy, but this will be diminished with design paste, paint, and glitter later.

4. Apply a layer of design paste over the pumpkin's facial features, using a gloved fingertip to smooth out rough surfaces. Allow to dry. Apply 2 coats of gesso to the outside of the pumpkin, allowing to dry between coats.

5. Tear tissue paper into 2" to 3" pieces and decoupage to the interior of the pumpkin, using Mod Podge and following manufacturer's directions. Cut away excess paper around the top edge of the pumpkin and smooth flat with your finger. Allow to dry. Repeat with the orange mulberry paper.

6. Apply 2 to 3 coats of Tangerine paint to the exterior of the pumpkin using the #20 shader brush, allowing to dry between coats. Apply White Wash paint to the eyes, Cadmium Orange to the nose, and French Vanilla to the mouth using the angular shader.

7. Trim the middle eye section and the teeth from the pattern. Tape the middle eye patterns in place on the pumpkin and trace the outlines with a pencil. Tape the mouth pattern without teeth to the pumpkin and trace teeth onto the pumpkin with a pencil.

8. Paint the middle eye area French Vanilla and paint teeth White Wash using the angular shader. Allow to dry. Outline the outer and middle eye areas using the filbert brush, and paint the smallest circle of the eye with Lamp Black using the angular shader. Outline points of teeth with Lamp Black. Allow to dry. Paint a ⅛" outline around the mouth with Cadmium Orange using the #0 shader brush. Allow to dry.

9. Apply glue to the surface of the pumpkin using the large glue brush and avoiding the facial details. Put on dust mask. Work in small sections at a time. Immediately sprinkle Tangerine glitter over the glue, shaking excess off onto scrap paper and then back into its container. Repeat until half the pumpkin is covered in glitter. Allow to dry, and then continue in same manner until the entire outer surface is covered with glitter.

10. Working with a single detail at a time and the small glue brush, apply glue to teeth and outer eye sections, covering black outlines, and then sprinkle with Glamour Dust. Shake off excess onto a piece of scrap paper and return to its container. Allow to dry.

11. Apply glue to the remaining area of the mouth, working with small sections at a time. Sprinkle Poupon glitter over the glue, shaking excess off onto a piece of scrap paper and then back into its container. Add Poupon glitter to the middle eye sections in the same manner. Allow to dry. Apply glue to large black eye circles and sprinkle with Black glitter, shaking excess onto scrap paper and then back into its container. Allow to dry.

12. Outline eyes and teeth again with Lamp Black paint to darken lines. Apply glue to the outline of the mouth. Sprinkle with Florida Orange glitter, shaking excess onto scrap paper and then back into its container.

13. Glue wooden tassel heads to each side of the wooden bead with wood glue, making a slight arc for the handle. Allow to dry. Paint with Cadmium Orange. Allow to dry. Apply glue to handle and sprinkle with Florida Orange glitter, shaking excess onto scrap paper and then back into its container. Allow to dry.

14. Using the awl, punch ⅛" holes, centered on each side of the pumpkin, ½" from the top. Repeat ¼" below the first holes. Insert glue into the holes with a toothpick. Position eyelets in the holes. Thread a 3" length of 22-gauge wire through the eyelets to the inside of the pumpkin, and twist on the inside to pull eyelets into position. Allow to set until glue is dry, and then remove wire.

15. Cut the length of 16-gauge black wire in half. Curve both pieces into an arc shape. Insert wires into the holes in the wooden handle and slide the handle to the center of the arc shape. Using round-nose pliers, make a loop at one wire end; then continue coiling wire to make a coil of about ⅝". Repeat at the remaining 3 wire ends.

16. Hold both coiled wires together at the ends. Wrap 22-gauge wire around both wires 5 times just above the coils and twist together on the back side to secure. Repeat at the other end. Insert the ends of the wire into the eyelet holes and then, on the inside of the pumpkin, insert ends into holes of button. Take a stitch across button with each wire and insert ends back down through remaining hole to back of button. Pull wires snug, removing excess slack. Tightly wrap wire ends around back of button a couple times and clip excess.

17. Cut a circle of felt to fit the bottom of the pumpkin without showing at the edges. Glue in place with tacky glue.

By Livia McRee

# GEL CAULDRON CANDLES

*Candle gel is the perfect choice for making these festive "bubbling" cauldrons. You can find mini-cauldrons at cooking supply stores and through mail-order catalogs. These are from Lodge (see "Sources" on page 95).*

## MATERIALS *(for 2 candles)*

- One 8.8-oz. package of emerald candle gel with wicks (Delta)
- Two 8.8-oz packages of yellow candle gel with wicks (Delta)
- Delta Gel Candle scent
- Two 3" x 5" cast-iron mini-cauldrons (Lodge)
- 2-cup glass measuring cup
- Scissors
- Saucepan
- Dish soap
- Kitchen towel
- 2 pencils
- Candy thermometer
- Metal spoon

## ◆ ◆ ◆ ◆ TIPS ◆ ◆ ◆ ◆

- Use a candy thermometer when melting wax to ensure you don't overheat it, which could cause it to catch fire.
- Peel wax residue from the saucepan after it cools and save for future candlemaking or discard in a trash receptacle. Do not wash it down the drain as the wax is not water soluble.
- Follow the manufacturer's safety precautions for burning your candle.

## INSTRUCTIONS

1. If using a cauldron that is different from the one shown here, determine how many ounces your container will hold by filling it with water and pouring the water into a measuring cup. Measure out that much gel, plus a little extra. To do this easily, snip the gel into pieces with scissors and then put the pieces in a measuring cup until the measurement equals the amount of water your cauldron holds. Take into account that you will leave ¼" to ½" of space at the top of the cauldron. For the cauldrons shown here you will need one package of yellow and half a package of emerald for each candle. Put the gel in a saucepan.

2. Prepare the cauldrons by washing them with dish soap and drying them. Insert wick into each cauldron so end just touches bottom. Tie the other end of the wick around a pencil and lay the pencil across the top of the container. Adjust as necessary so there is no slack in the wick.

3. Melt the gel over very low heat, stirring frequently to dissolve lumps. This will take only 10 to 15 minutes. Use the candy thermometer to ensure that the gel does not overheat; it should not exceed 205°F.

4. When the temperature cools to 180°F, add 3 to 5 drops of scent per ounce of gel. Be sure to use scent formulated for candle gel. Stir well with a metal spoon.

5. Candle gel is ready to pour at 180°F, once all the chunks have dissolved. Pour it carefully and slowly into the cauldrons, leaving at least ¼" of space from the top of the container. Once the candles have solidified, which will take about 2 hours, trim the wicks to ¼" above the surface.

BY GENEVIEVE A. STERBENZ

# HAUNTED TREE DECORATION

*Impress trick-or-treaters and holiday guests alike with this eerie haunted tree decoration. This simple assemblage combines an aged stone urn dripping with Spanish moss with a gnarled branch strewn with spider webs, a couple of black crows, and the last surviving leaves of fall. This arrangement works equally well displayed on a wall indoors or hung outside on your front door.*

## MATERIALS

- 16" x 8" x 6½"-deep half urn
- 16" x 30" manzanita branch
- Spanish moss
- Decorative spider webbing
- 7 pairs of silk leaves in fall colors
- 2 black crows
- Kraft paper
- Drill and drill bit
- Ruler
- Heavy picture-hanging wire
- Wire cutters
- Floral tape
- Floral clay
- Floral foam blocks
- Serrated knife
- Scissors
- Glue gun and glue sticks
- 3 picture hooks
- Fishing line

## TIP

I used a half urn (an urn with one flat side) that I found at a small local garden-supply store. If you are not able to find one, consider making this arrangement using a footed free-standing urn and placing it on the floor. I found the best way to work with the half urn was to set it on a low table, such as a coffee table, up against a wall. The low surface keeps the arrangement within reach while you work, and with the urn propped up you can ensure that the branch is placed far enough forward so that the arrangement will hang flush against a wall or door.

## INSTRUCTIONS

1. Cover a clean, flat work surface with kraft paper. Drill 2 holes in the urn from the back, about 2" from each end. Cut an 18" length of wire and run 1 end through the first hole, along the inside of urn, and out through the second hole. Bring the ends together on the outside back of the urn and twist together. Set aside.

2. Wrap the bottom 4" of the branch with floral tape. Make a ball approximately the size of an egg from floral clay.

3. Adhere the ball of floral clay to the bottom of the branch and position the branch in the bottom of the urn. Hold the branch and urn up against a flat surface to find the proper positioning. Mold clay around the bottom of the branch and to the bottom of the urn, adding more clay if necessary to secure. To fill the urn with floral foam, place a block on the right side of the branch and press down onto the top edges of the urn, creating an imprint in the foam. Using a serrated knife, cut foam along imprinted lines and set aside any excess. Place the foam in the bottom of the urn. Repeat for the left side. Continue adding pieces of foam until the urn is filled and the foam is flush with the top edges of the urn.

4. Tuck Spanish moss into spaces between the pieces of foam to secure in place. Let some moss cascade over the front and sides of the urn. To add spider webs, cut a 3" length of stretchable spider webbing. Beginning at one end, start pulling the webbing apart. Hook the stretched end onto a lower branch, and then pull the webbing up to a higher branch and hook again to secure. Continue moving webbing from branch to branch, or cut to begin in a new spot.

5. To add leaves, slide the plastic ring at the base of leaves onto a narrow offshoot of the manzanita branch and secure in place using a glue gun. Continue adding leaves the same way, as desired (see project photo on page 92). To add crows, twist wire at the base of the crows' feet around the branch. Secure with a drop of hot glue on the back side of the branch, if necessary.

6. Mark 3 spots on the wall or door where you plan to hang the decoration: 2 in line with the wire at the back of the urn and 1 directly behind the midsection of the branch. Secure picture hooks to the hanging surface at the marked points. Hang the wire on the back of the urn from the 2 bottom hooks. Wrap a length of fishing line around the center of the branch and tie both ends around the remaining hook to secure.

# SOURCES

**Delphi Stained Glass**
800-248-2048 or 517-394-4631
www.delphiglass.com
Stained glass
(Spooky Glass Coasters, page 23;
Mosaic Pumpkin Lantern, page 66)

**Impress Rubber Stamps**
206-901-9101
www.impressrubberstamps.com
Background rubber stamp,
snaps for party crackers
(Halloween Invitations, page 7;
Halloween Party Crackers, page 34)

**Lodge Manufacturing Company**
423-837-7181
www.lodgemfg.com
Cauldrons
(Gel Cauldron Candles, page 91)

**Sam Flax**
www.samflax.com
Frisket film
(Haunted House Ice Bucket, page 15)

**Stained Glass Warehouse, Inc.**
828-650-0982
www.stainedglasswarehouse.com
Stained glass
(Spooky Glass Coasters, page 23;
Mosaic Pumpkin Lantern, page 66)

**Warner Crivellaro**
800-623-4242
www.warner-criv.com
Stained glass
(Spooky Glass Coasters, page 23;
Mosaic Pumpkin Lantern, page 66)

# new and bestselling titles from

America's Best-Loved Craft & Hobby Books®

America's Best-Loved Quilt Books®

## NEW RELEASES
1000 Great Quilt Blocks
Basically Brilliant Knits
Bright Quilts from Down Under
Christmas Delights
Creative Machine Stitching
Crochet for Tots
Crocheted Aran Sweaters
Cutting Corners
Everyday Embellishments
Folk Art Friends
Garden Party
Hocus Pocus!
Just Can't Cut It!
Quilter's Home: Winter, The
Sweet and Simple Baby Quilts
Time to Quilt
Today's Crochet
Traditional Quilts to Paper Piece

## APPLIQUÉ
Appliquilt in the Cabin
Artful Album Quilts
Artful Appliqué
Blossoms in Winter
Color-Blend Appliqué
Sunbonnet Sue All through the Year

## BABY QUILTS
Easy Paper-Pieced Baby Quilts
Even More Quilts for Baby
More Quilts for Baby
Play Quilts
Quilted Nursery, The
Quilts for Baby

## HOLIDAY QUILTS & CRAFTS
Christmas Cats and Dogs
Creepy Crafty Halloween
Handcrafted Christmas, A
Make Room for Christmas Quilts
Welcome to the North Pole

## HOME DECORATING
Decorated Kitchen, The
Decorated Porch, The
Dresden Fan
Gracing the Table
Make Room for Quilts
Quilts for Mantels and More
Sweet Dreams

## LEARNING TO QUILT
101 Fabulous Rotary-Cut Quilts
Beyond the Blocks
Casual Quilter, The
Feathers That Fly
Joy of Quilting, The
Simple Joys of Quilting, The
Your First Quilt Book (or it should be!)

## PAPER PIECING
40 Bright and Bold Paper-Pieced Blocks
50 Fabulous Paper-Pieced Stars
For the Birds
Quilter's Ark, A
Rich Traditions
Split-Diamond Dazzlers

## ROTARY CUTTING
365 Quilt Blocks a Year Perpetual Calendar
Around the Block Again
Around the Block with Judy Hopkins
Fat Quarter Quilts
More Fat Quarter Quilts
Stack the Deck!
Triangle Tricks
Triangle-Free Quilts

## SCRAP QUILTS
Nickel Quilts
Scrap Frenzy
Scrappy Duos
Spectacular Scraps
Strips and Strings
Successful Scrap Quilts

## TOPICS IN QUILTMAKING
American Stenciled Quilts
Americana Quilts
Batik Beauties
Bed and Breakfast Quilts
Fabulous Quilts from Favorite Patterns
Frayed-Edge Fun
Patriotic Little Quilts
Reversible Quilts

## CRAFTS
ABCs of Making Teddy Bears, The
Blissful Bath, The
Handcrafted Frames
Handcrafted Garden Accents
Handprint Quilts
Painted Chairs
Painted Whimsies

## KNITTING & CROCHET
365 Knitting Stitches a Year Perpetual
    Calendar
Clever Knits
Crochet for Babies and Toddlers
Crocheted Sweaters
Knitted Sweaters for Every Season
Knitted Throws and More
Knitter's Book of Finishing Techniques, Th
Knitter's Template, A
More Paintbox Knits
Paintbox Knits
Too Cute! Cotton Knits for Toddlers
Treasury of Rowan Knits, A
Ultimate Knitter's Guide, The

Our books are available at bookstores and your favorite craft, fabric, and yarn retailers. If you don't see the title you're looking for, visit us at **www.martingale-pub.com** or contact us at:

## 1-800-426-3126

International: 1-425-483-3313

Fax: 1-425-486-7596

Email: info@martingale-pub.com

For more information and a full list of our titles, visit our Web site.